Museums of Southern California

Museums of Southern California

Sara LeBien

PEREGRINE SMITH BOOKS
SALT LAKE CITY

First edition

92 91 90 89 88   5 4 3 2 1

Copyright © 1988 Gibbs Smith, Publisher

This is a Peregrine Smith Book
Published by Gibbs Smith, Publisher
P.O. Box 667, Layton, UT 84041

Design by Donna Hewitt

Printed and bound in the United States of
America

Library of Congress Cataloging-in-Publication
Data

LeBien, Sara.
   Museums of Southern California.
   Includes index.
   1. Museums—California, Southern—
Guide—books. 2. California, Southern—
Description and travel—Guide-books. I. Title.
AM12.C2L43   1988   917.94'9   88-12424
ISBN 0-87905-325-9

This book is dedicated to my husband,
Bob, who first suggested that I write it,
believed in it as much as I did,
and then encouraged me every step of the way.

Contents

Acknowledgments

I wish both to thank and pay tribute to the hundreds of volunteers who provide numerous services in the everyday workings of a museum: organizing huge mailings, serving as docents, working in gift shops, typing labels, cleaning windows, and tending the flower arrangements. These are dedicated community supporters who believe in the importance of museums and willingly give their time, talents, and material contributions. We are all deeply indebted to them.

I wish to thank my typist, Terri Landis, for her cheerful nature and efficient help, and Mona Letourneau for her initial guidance. To my editor, Leslie Cutler Stitt, I wish to express my appreciation for her enthusiasm for the project, her meticulous attention to detail, and her thoughtful regard for my satisfaction with the outcome of the book.

Preface

One morning my husband Bob and I were wondering what kind of museum we wanted to visit that day. Unable to make up our minds, it occurred to us that a guidebook to southern California museums would be very handy just then. Our plans for the day evolved into a trip to the library, and the beginning of this book. It is intended as a guide for anyone who frequents museums, as well as for occasional museum-goers, whether they are children or adults, scouts or scholars, collectors or the curious. Most museum-goers only visit well-known museums. This guidebook describes some of the special programs and offerings at these major museums, but also introduces many minor museums that are well worth visiting. The number of museums there are in southern California will surprise many, and a selection of more than 170, between Santa Barbara and San Diego, is described in this guide.

In sprawling California, where one often drives quite a distance to visit a good museum, it is disappointing to realize afterward that one missed a museum that was right around the corner. First-time visitors to the George C. Page Museum of the La Brea Discoveries may not know that the Craft and Folk Art Museum is just across the street. Visitors to the University of California Santa Barbara Art Museum can also visit the historic Stow House and Goleta Depot Railroad Museum directly across the freeway. The handy indexes in this guide will help tourists, residents, and California newcomers to plan fuller museum outings and holidays. Since museums occasionally change hours and admission prices, and close briefly while new exhibitions are installed, it is recommended that visitors call first.

The museums have been grouped together and placed into chapters based on the geography of an area, county lines, and the accessibility of freeways. Chapter 1, with twenty–two museums listed, includes downtown Los Angeles, and the area south of the Santa Monica Freeway (I–10) down to Compton. It also goes east to the

City of Industry. Chapter 2—Mid-Wilshire and the West Side— encompasses Beverly Hills, Westwood, Santa Monica, and Malibu, and notes thirteen museums. The South Bay area stretches from Lomita to Long Beach, includes fourteen museums, and comprises Chapter 3. Chapter 4 includes five museums in the coastal area of Orange County, from Newport Beach to Dana Point. Chapter 5—ten museums—is the inland area of Orange County beginning at La Habra and including Buena Park, Fullerton, Placentia, Anaheim, Santa Ana, and El Toro. Chapter 6 with twenty-five museums of the La Jolla and San Diego area also includes Vista and the Imperial Valley. The twenty museums in Riverside and San Bernardino counties comprise Chapter 7, and span an area reaching from Chino and Ontario east to Yucca Valley, north to Barstow, and southeast to Palm Springs. Chapter 8 of the San Gabriel Valley, begins in Pasadena and goes east to Claremont, staying north of the San Bernardino Freeway (I-10). There are twelve museums in this section. The nine museums in Chapter 9 are located in the condensed Hollywood and Griffith Park area which stays south of Ventura Freeway (134), west of Golden State Freeway (I-5) and mostly east of the Hollywood Freeway (101). Chapter 10 of the San Fernando Valley and Antelope Valley spans a large area beginning in Glendale, reaching north to Mojave and west to Calabasas, and includes eighteen museums. Chapter 11 contains the area of Thousand Oaks north to Santa Barbara and Goleta. The twenty-three museums are very diverse in nature and are located mainly in the coastal towns with one each in inland Simi, Fillmore, and Ojai.

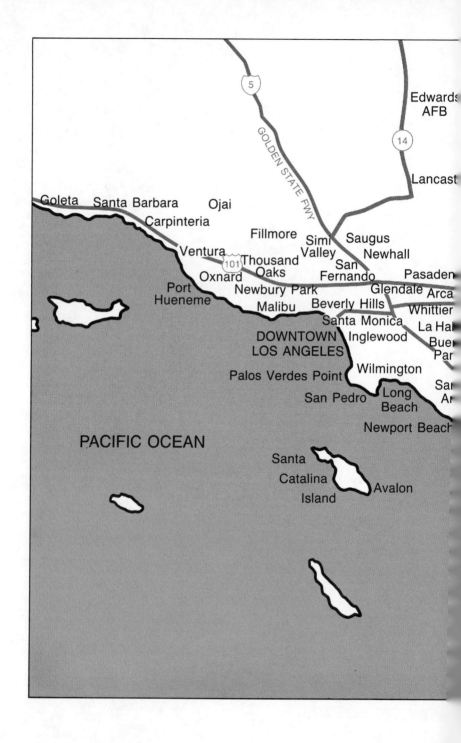

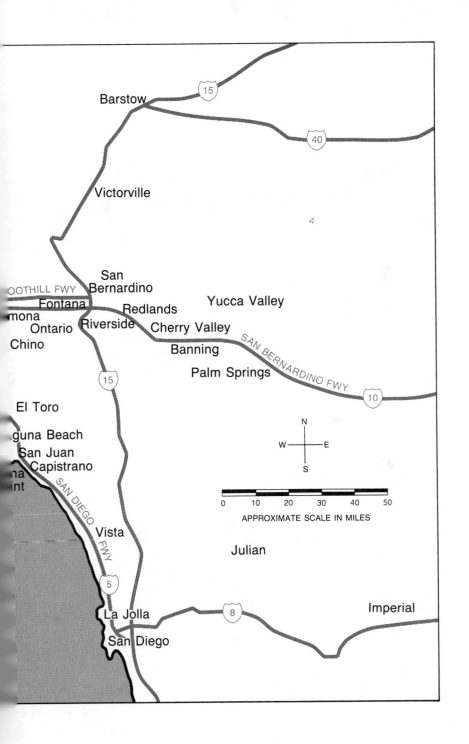

Chapter One

Downtown Los Angeles and Communities to the South and East

American Heritage Park / Military Museum

1918 North Rosemead Blvd., South El Monte, CA 91733

GETTING THERE: From the Pomona Fwy (60), take Rosemead Blvd. exit and go north 3/4 mile.

Adjacent to the Whittier Narrows Recreation Area in El Monte is a seven and one-half acre outdoor military "parking lot" of military vehicles. It has the largest interservice (Army, Navy, Marine Corps, and Air Force) military collection in the West, and some foreign vehicles. A new feature being developed is a replica of the "M.A.S.H. 4077" set, with helicopter, tents, and hospital. The museum restores old equipment from the government and private donors to working order before they are displayed in the park. Also on view are German cars made by Volkswagen, a German light antiaircraft, American and German antitank guns, a 1930s MI combat car, ambulances, cargo trucks, jeeps, staff car, and a Vietnamese riverboat for laying mines. Visitors should not expect typical museum-type displays or attractive park grounds, but those interested in military vehicles will enjoy it. No restaurant, drinking fountains, or restroom facilities. Self-guided tours. Wheelchair access. Parking on premises.

The main office of the American Heritage Park is in Patriotic Hall at 1816 South Figueroa Street in Los Angeles. Headquartered in this military affairs building are one hundred military organizations and interesting small exhibits of military artifacts on each floor.

1

Open Saturday and Sunday noon–4:30 P.M. Closed during rainy weather. Admission is $2 for adults, $1 for children 10 and older, 50¢ for children under 10. For more information call Park/Museum (818) 442-1776 or Patriotic Hall (213) 746-1776.

The Bailey House
13421 East Camilla St., Whittier, CA 90601

GETTING THERE: From the Whittier Blvd. exit on the San Gabriel River Fwy (I-605), go east on Whittier Blvd. to Pickering Ave. Turn north, go to Camilla St. and turn east.

This home of Whittier's first settlers, Jonathan and Rebecca Bailey, is a landmark of the Quaker heritage and the early history of Whittier. The first Quaker meetings, attended by only ten people, were conducted on the front porch, and later the house became the center of Whittier's business, social, and religious activity. The furnishings of the 1865–1904 period include many of the original items and Bailey family mementos. Children visiting this house will especially enjoy seeing the dry sink and working water pump in the kitchen, the ornate Victorian wicker baby carriage with its attached silk umbrella, and the living room portiere that resembles a macrame hanging but on close inspection proves to be eucalyptus pods.

Tours available. Christmas tea held annually. Museum programs, special events, and tours to other historic sites. School tours. No restaurant. No wheelchair access. Street parking.

Open Sunday 1–4 P.M. Admission is 50¢ for adults, 25¢ for visitors under 18. For more information call the Whittier Historical Society at (213) 945-3871.

California Museum of Afro-American History and Culture
Exposition Park, 600 State Dr., Los Angeles, CA 90037

GETTING THERE: From the Harbor Fwy (I-110) take the Martin Luther King, Jr. Blvd. exit (Santa Barbara Blvd.) and go west to Figueroa St. Turn right onto Figueroa and left into museum parking next to the Aerospace Museum.

This museum of Afro-American art and artifacts is housed in a handsome, one-level contemporary structure designed by two Los

Angeles architects, Jack Haywood and Vincent Proby. Visitors enter a 13,000-square-foot sculpture court and gallery showing works by Afro-American artists from 1800s to the present. Extending from the main exhibition space are three smaller galleries that highlight visiting exhibitions and the museum's permanent collection of paintings, collage, and sculpture ranging from realist to naive.

Dedicated to collecting and preserving artifacts documenting the Afro-American experience, the museum has an extensive collection of works by the Haitian painter F. Turenne de Pres and early graphite drawings by Edward Mitchell Bannister. The modern collection features Herman (Kofi) Bailey, Romare Bearden, Herbert Gentry, and Jacob Lawrence. Sculpture is represented by John Wilson, Richard Barthe, Carroll Harris Simms, John Outerbridge, Mel Edwards, Barbara Chase-Ribound, Maren Hassinger, and John Riddle. Mixed-media assemblages are by Noah Purifoy, Marie Johnson-Calloway, and David Hammons. Early American paintings are by James Porter, Clementine Hunter, Ernie Barnes, and Charles Sebree. Martinique and West African artifacts, photographs, and literary artifacts such as books and documents are also part of the permanent collection.

The museum offers many educational services. Docent visits to schools as well as educational kits and school tours are available. Special programs include films, Children's Film Festival, lectures, national traveling exhibitions, multimedia presentations, workshops, and performing arts. The open court with its high ceiling provides a viewing area during the day and an ideal space for receptions and performances in the evening. Additional facilities include a research library and archives, meeting hall, and theater. Toys, cookbooks, masks, art and black history books, contemporary jewelry, posters, and cards are available in the gift shop. A McDonald's is located in Exposition Park. Picnic area. Wheelchair access. Docent tours are available at no charge.

Open daily 10 A.M.–5 P.M. Closed Memorial Day, Thanksgiving, Christmas, and New Year's Day. Free admission and parking. For more information and to reserve tours call (213) 744-7432.

3

California Museum of Science and Industry
700 State Dr., Los Angeles, CA 90037

California Museum of Science and Industry
Aerospace Museum
IMAX Theater
Mark Taper Hall of Economics and Finance
Kinsey Hall of Health Sciences

GETTING THERE: From the Harbor Fwy (I-110), take the Exposition Blvd. exit west to Menlo Ave. Turn left into Exposition Park. From the Santa Monica Fwy (I-10), take the Vermont Ave. exit, go south to Exposition Blvd. Turn east and follow to Menlo Ave. Turn left into Exposition Park.

The complex consists of four museums and a theater. After a $55 million renovation prior to the 1984 Olympics, this has become an exciting participatory and hands-on museum complex, ranked as one of America's largest science and technology museums and second only to the Smithsonian.

Nineteen different school tours are provided for all age groups. Special parent-child classes are offered including "Exploring Science on Saturdays" and "Electric Company." Class workshop themes change yearly and have included "Discovering the Arid Earth," "The Terrific Science Factory," and "Advanced Rocketry." A children's summer workshop and special opportunities for competition and research with professionals are also offered.

The museum complex also hosts the county and state science fairs. For more information call (213) 744-7438. Two gift shops on the premises. A McDonald's is located within the complex. Wheelchair access is available throughout. Free limited parking at the museums and near Figueroa.

All buildings open daily 9 A.M.–5 P.M. Free admission. For more information call (213) 744-7400 and to reserve tours call (213) 744-7470.

California Museum of Science and Industry
The complex takes its name from this museum housed in the old brick building which was the original structure. One of the most popular features is the largest earthquake simulator in the U.S. open to the public, permitting about twenty visitors at a time to

An energy exhibit at the Museum of Science and Industry captivates grade-schoolers and Sgt. Beepo, one of the museum's Methanians. *Courtesy California Museum of Science and Industry.*

experience the sound and feel of a major earthquake. Question-and-answer displays test the visitor's understanding of practical knowledge about earthquake precautions to take during and after an earthquake. One major exhibition area explains computer languages and how to use them, and also demonstrates computer graphics. The history of photography is the subject of another exhibit, and California industries are featured in a large agriculture section housing a chick hatchery and other displays. In addition to these innovative permanent installations several major shows are presented annually.

The Museum of Science and Industry offers tours and year-round science workshops. Call (213) 744-7440. Smithsonian lecture and seminar program and live skits within the exhibits are at scheduled showtimes. The gift shop has an exciting array of model electronic robot kits, microcomputer robots, holograms, hologram art, kaleidoscopes, space shuttle kits, a sixteen-inch earth-in-space globe, and many science toys.

Aerospace Museum
The modern building connected to the Museum of Science and Industry is the Aerospace Museum. Divided into three main areas, this comprehensive space museum has exhibits pertaining to the universe, satellites, and flight. One exhibit features mankind's exploration of the solar system, and a satellite area has participatory exhibits permitting visitors to tap into a national weather satellite or call up satellite images of the earth's crust or the ocean floor. There is also a flight area where visitors can see a graphic presentation of the history of flight. Participatory and hands-on displays demonstrate the principles of flight. Bridges and balconies enable visitors to get close to the full-size models suspended from the high ceiling (its highest point is equivalent to seven stories).

This $4 million building also houses the actual Gemini II spacecraft, a T-38 Air Force trainer, a VELA satellite, and a 1928 Monocoupe airplane. An F-104 Star Fighter is displayed prominently outside the building. The Aerospace complex includes the Space Terrace, Corwin D. Denney Air and Space Garden (the location of the DC-8 and DC-3), and the IMAX Theater. The Aerospace gift shop sells space-related books, gift items, and toys.

IMAX Theater
The IMAX is a science and technology theater. A five-story film screen, one of the largest ever built, and state-of-the-art technology are used to present several films famed for making viewers feel as if they are part of the action. These include *The Dream is Alive,* a space shuttle trip; *We Are Born of Stars,* a story of the universe; *Sacred Site,* a worldwide travelog; *Grand Canyon: The Hidden Secrets; Chronos,* a story of western civilization; and *Behold Hawaii.* Films are subject to change. Wheelchair access.

Hourly films from 10 A.M.–8 P.M. For tickets call (213) 744-2014. Group rates available. For more information call (213) 744-2019.

Mark Taper Hall of Economics and Finance
A tribute to the free enterprise system, the Mark Taper Hall of Economics and Finance is the only museum in the U.S. devoted exclusively to economics. The 27,000-square-foot space provides a high-involvement environment with hundreds of buttons and levers to manipulate. More than sixty computers explain and illustrate basic principles of economics and finance. A computer card is used here in exhibits and games about money, banking, and the national debt. An economics IQ test can be lots of fun.

Kinsey Hall of Health Sciences
Kinsey Hall of Health Sciences has participatory exhibits where visitors discover ways to improve their own health and nutrition. Using a computer card, visitors check their own breathing rates as well as heart rate, pulse, stress level, and other vital signs, and, before leaving, receive a computerized printout politely summing up the participant's health profile. Other fascinating displays explain human reproduction, the five senses, and how drugs and narcotics work.

Centinela Adobe
7634 Midfield Ave., Inglewood, CA 90045

GETTING THERE: Take the San Diego Fwy (I–405) to the La Cienega Blvd. exit. Go west on Florence and north on Hindry. Turn right on 82nd St. and follow the curve to Midfield.

This former residence of Daniel Freeman, the founder of Inglewood, contains Victorian home furnishings, business and

Sixty-two exhibits, such as this one on money, bring life to economic concepts at the Mark Taper Hall of Economics and Finance. Courtesy California Museum of Science and Industry.

farm tools, photographs, and family memorabilia. There are three buildings on the site: an adobe-style house built in 1834, a land office, and a research center. The land office, built in 1887, is furnished with business and farm tools of that era. The new Heritage and Research Center houses a library and storage facility for artifacts. Tours available. Call (213) 677-7916. An annual barbecue is held in June, a fiesta in September, and a Christmas open house in December featuring caroling and lighted *candelarios*. No restaurant or shop. Wheelchair access.

Open Wednesday and Sunday 2–4 P.M. Free admission and parking. A donation is appreciated. For more information call (213) 649-6272.

Dominguez Rancho Adobe (Dominguez Seminary)
18127 South Alameda St., Compton, CA 90220

GETTING THERE: From Los Angeles take the Harbor Fwy (I–110) south to the Artesia Fwy (91). Go east on 91 to the Alameda exit. Follow the exit lane on the right to turn right on Alameda. The entrance to the seminary is ¼ mile south of 91.

This structure was a significant site in California's early history. Juan José Dominguez was a Spanish soldier in an exploratory expedition that marched into San Diego in 1769, who then spent the next twenty years protecting Father Junipero Serra and other Franciscan padres during the establishment of the California mission chain. After he retired, Dominguez was given 75,000 acres of land. It was the first land concession made in southern California under the Spanish empire.

The adobe has a colorful history. Dominguez's grand-nephew, Manuel Dominguez, an important civic leader and one of the framers of the state constitution, inherited the property, built the residence, and resided here for fifty-five years. During the Mexican War the U.S. marines occupied the house briefly, and it served as a political meeting house and overnight lodge for stagecoach travelers en route between San Pedro and Los Angeles. In 1934 it was donated to the Clarentian Missionaries, and in 1976 the original six rooms were designated a historical museum.

9

On view today is a family sitting room still furnished as a chapel, a large kitchen, bedrooms containing the original mission period furniture, mementos, and clothing. A collection of model railroads is also on display. One room houses an exhibition of the 1910 Dominguez air meet held on Dominguez Hill. Picnic areas and limited wheelchair access. Call in advance for guided tour reservations for groups of ten or more.

Open Tuesday and Wednesday 1–4 P.M. Free admission and parking. For more information, call (213) 631–5981 or (213) 636–6030.

Downey Museum of Art
10419 South Rives Ave., Downey, CA 90241

GETTING THERE: From Los Angeles, take the Santa Ana Fwy (I–5) to Paramount Blvd. exit. Continue south to Florence Ave. Turn right (west), go to Rives Ave. Turn left (south) and go to Furman Park. The museum is located on park grounds.

Artists of the twentieth century are the main attraction here. An interesting new show opens every six weeks with a focus on contemporary art. Past shows have included "Contemporary Metals U.S.A. II" representing artists from thirty-eight states with exhibits of jewelry, abstract welded steel, a 200-pound gate, crocheted silver wire nine feet high, Nairobian sculpture, and a ninety-one-pound apple. Four major thematic shows are held annually and feature glass art, ceramics, metal sculpture, and jewelry. Tours available, reservations necessary. Films and lectures. Annual art fair in the park. Art programs by arrangement for schools. Wheelchair access.

Open Wednesday–Sunday noon–5 P.M. Admission is $1 for adults, 50¢ for senior citizens, children free. Special juried art shows have admission fee. For a recorded message call (213) 861–0419 and for more information and to reserve tours call (213) 928–8609.

El Pueblo de Los Angeles State Historic Park
845 North Alameda St., Los Angeles, CA 90012

GETTING THERE: Located in downtown Los Angeles. Traveling south on the Hollywood Fwy (U.S. 101) take the Los Angeles St. or Alameda exit. Turn left. Traveling north on 101, exit at Alameda, turn right, and follow signs.

Rustic cart carreta. *Courtesy El Pueblo de Los Angeles Historic Park. Photo by Sara LeBien.*

Early nineteenth-century steam engine. Courtesy El Pueblo de Los Angeles State Historic Park. Photo by Frank Thomas.

Visitors to Los Angeles and residents alike will enjoy visiting Olvera Street to shop in the colorful plaza, eat Mexican food, and enjoy the festive atmosphere, many without knowing that this area is the birthplace of Los Angeles. Eleven Indian, Spanish, black and mixed-heritage families first settled here. The original huts are gone, but twenty-seven historical structures, built later during the colonial period, remain. Eleven are open to the public, four of which are restored as museums.

The Avila Adobe and Church of Our Lady of Angels were two of the first buildings here in the 1880s. The adobe is a fine example of California Hispanic life in the 1840s. Unfortunately, many visitors to Olvera Street are so captivated by its shops and restaurants that the adobe may not always be noticed.

Directly across the walkway of market stalls is Sepulveda House, a two-story Victorian structure. There is a visitors center on the first floor. Nearby is Our Lady of Angels, the oldest church in Los Angeles which is still active. The city's first Masonic Hall was erected in the 1860s, and among its memorabilia are the propeller blade from Eddie Rickenbaker's airplane and the rope from the rigging of the life raft in which he drifted for twenty-four days in the Pacific during World War II.

Also on view are the façades of Pico House, a hotel built by the last Mexican governor of California, Pio Pico, and the Merced Hotel next door. The first firehouse in Los Angeles, built in the 1880s, also on site, is meticulously furnished with period furniture and equipment. The Garnier block area was once a neighborhood to Chinese railroad workers, and the city's first Chinatown.

Twenty-two other historic buildings in El Pueblo are also on view. Guided tours available. Tour map available. Several restaurants in plaza. Wheelchair access, parking, and ramps. Parking at nominal fee, or $3–$4 daily. Gift shop.

The plaza is open daily. Avila Adobe is open Tuesday–Friday 10 A.M.–3 P.M. and 10 A.M.–4:30 P.M. on weekends. Sepulveda House is open Monday–Friday 10 A.M.–3 P.M. and 10 A.M.–4:30 P.M. on Saturday. Closed Sundays. The church is open daily. The firehouse is open Tuesday–Friday 10 A.M.–3 P.M. and 10 A.M.–4:30 P.M. on weekends. The Masonic Hall is open Tuesday-Friday 10 A.M.–3 P.M. Admission is free. For more information call (213) 628-1274 or (213) 628-7170.

Heritage Square
3800 Homer St., Highland Park, Los Angeles, CA 90031

GETTING THERE: Heading north on Pasadena Fwy (I–110), take the Avenue 43 exit and go right.

Heritage Square is a ten-acre parcel of land that is being developed into a beautiful Victorian neighborhood. Eight historical structures built between 1865 and 1915 now stand on the property, and future plans include a Victorian bandstand, a horse-car line, original railway cars from Angels Flight in downtown Los Angeles, and a commercial section featuring an ice cream parlor, general store, restaurant, and museum. This living museum is within a few blocks of the Southwest Museum, Casa de Adobe, and the Lummis Home, and its grounds and historic buildings are well worth a visit.

Hale House, circa 1887. This beautiful house contains ornate chimneys, stained-glass windows, and extensive exterior carvings in Queen Anne and Westlake style.

Mount Pleasant House, circa 1876. An Italianate former home of two business and cultural leaders.

Valley Knudsen Garden Residence, circa 1883. One of the few surviving examples of nineteenth-century mansard architecture. A rare coral tree, the official tree of Los Angeles, flourishes by this residence.

Carriage Barn, circa 1899. Combines Queen Anne Cottage and Gothic styles.

Lincoln Ave. Methodist Church, circa 1897. An example of Gothic style with detailed pediments and gables of the Queen Anne and Eastlake styles.

Beaudry Street House, circa 1887. Former residence of John Ford, a well-known wood carver. Combines styles of Italianate, Eastlake, and Queen Anne periods with Ford's extensive interior and exterior hand-carved detailing.

Palms Depot, circa 1885. Served Los Angeles railroad passengers for more than six decades.

Octagon House. This former Pasadena residence is currently being restored.

Heritage Square's event of the year is the annual "Victorian Christmas Faire," with music, entertainment, food, and Christmas gift shopping. For tours call (818) 480–0654, 1–4 P.M. one month in advance for a group tour application. Mrs. Shaw's Emporium gift shop sells Victorian reproductions. No restaurants on location. No wheelchair facilities or access.

Open Saturday and Sunday 11 A.M.–4 P.M. Admission is $3 for adults, $2 for senior citizens, $2 for children 12–18, under 12 free. For more information call (818) 449–0193.

Los Angeles Children's Museum
310 North Main St., Los Angeles, CA 90013

GETTING THERE: The museum is located at Main and Aliso streets, next to the Hollywood Fwy. Southbound on the Hollywood Fwy (U.S. 101) take the Los Angeles St. exit or the Alameda-Union Station exit. Go past Alameda and turn left.

More like a funhouse than a museum, the Children's Museum is filled with color, excitement, and activity. There are hands-on exhibits and play areas with themes such as city life, colonial living, creativity, animation, technology, and crafts. Children can play at being camera operators or news reporters in a simulated television newsroom, or performers and technicians in a recording room, or they might try recycling factory odds and ends from a huge barrel into sculpture. Abundant craft workshops are often in progress. There are scheduled live performances and art, dance, and theater workshops on weekends.

Ever wonder what goes on underneath a city sidewalk? An exposed section reveals the answer. There are many stimulating displays throughout this hands-on, see-through, participatory museum. Both permanent and rotating exhibits are fun and educational. Tours. Gift shop. Fast food restaurants in the mall.

15

Underground parking, Monday–Saturday. Wheelchair access. Sunday parking at San Pedro and Temple streets.

Open Wednesday and Thursday 2–4 P.M. and weekends 10 A.M.–5 P.M. Admission is $4, under 2 years free. For more information call (213) 687–8801 or (213) 687–8800 for recorded message.

Charles F. Lummis Home—"El Alisal"
200 East Avenue 43, Highland Park, CA 90042

GETTING THERE: Take the Avenue 43 exit from Pasadena Fwy (I–110). Turn left and go one block to the house.

Charles F. Lummis was the first city editor of the *Los Angeles Times*, a founder of the Southwest Museum and a noted writer, archaeologist, historian, photographer, and western Americana enthusiast. He built his house by hand using local stones and lumber as well as discarded telegraph poles. Named "El Alisal," it is an eclectic composite of do-it-yourself Spanish and Southwest architecture. The house and its garden became the meeting place of southern California's culture colonists until Lummis's death in 1928.

Memorabilia, books, and photos of the Charles Fletcher Lummis family are featured as well as historical and cultural artifacts representing his interests in archaeology, ethnology, history, and Native Americans. Docent-led tours. Street parking. No restaurant. Wheelchair access.

Open Wednesday–Sunday 1–4 P.M. Admission is free. For more information call (213) 222–0546.

Museum of Contemporary Art (MOCA) and Temporary Contemporary (TC)
MOCA—250 South Grand Ave., California Plaza, Los Angeles, CA 90012
TC—152 North Central Ave., Los Angeles, CA 90012

GETTING TO MOCA: Accessible from the following freeways: Hollywood Fwy (U.S. 101), Pasadena Fwy (I–110), Santa Ana Fwy (I–5), and Santa Monica Fwy (I–10). The main entrance of the museum is on the upper level of Grand Ave. but the parking is entered below the building on the lower level of Grand Ave. The

A bird's-eye view of the Museum of Contemporary Art (MOCA) and sculpture,
The Knife Ship II, in the courtyard. Photo by Sara LeBien.

DASH shuttle service operating downtown makes stops near the California Plaza building at First St. and Grand Ave.

GETTING TO TC: From Harbor/Pasadena Fwy (I–110) take the First St. exit to Central Ave. From Hollywood Fwy (U.S. 101) take the Alameda St. or Los Angeles St. exit south to First St. Go east on First St. to Central Ave. Turn left. DASH makes a stop at First St. and San Pedro St.

"MOCA" and "TC" are nicknames for these fascinating contemporary art museums. The Museum of Contemporary Art (MOCA) was expected to be finished in time for the 1984 Olympics, but when delays prevented it, an alternative building was chosen to house the exhibits. The Temporary Contemporary (TC) opened in a run-down 55,000-square-foot police garage in Little Tokyo. After clever renovations by architect Frank Gehry, it has a series of changeable galleries and a steel-framed chainlink canopy extended out over the street to define the entrance. The TC proved to be so successful that its lease with the city was renewed for fifty years. So now there are two exhibition facilities.

MOCA finally opened in December 1986 in the downtown business district of California Plaza in the redeveloped Bunker Hill area. The 98,000-square-foot gallery complex was designed to attract people to its form and materials, which greatly contrast to the surrounding high-rise buildings. Museum architect Arata Isozaki described it as "a small village inside the valley created by the skyscrapers." The museum galleries comprise a single level of seven exhibition areas and an outdoor sculptor courtyard of 5,900 square feet for the display of outdoor works.

Devoted solely to contemporary art, the museum's permanent collection of 425 works and its visiting exhibitions focus on the period from 1940 to the present, with great interest in emerging California artists. Emphasis is on involving the general public in the understanding of contemporary art. The programs offer a wide range of "transmedia" or interdisciplinary arts exploring music, dance, performing arts, video, film, and poetry.

The permanent collection began with the acquisition of eighty major abstract expressionist and pop art pieces from the collection of Dr. and Mrs. Guiseppe Panza di Biumo. The collection comprises works of painting, print, sculpture, photography, and drawing by thirty-eight artists who represent minimalist works of the 1960s and 1970s, neo-expressionism, new image painting, post-minimalist, and post-modernist work of the 1980s. Major works by Louise Nevelson, Robert Irwin, James Turrell, and Douglas Wheeler represent the West Coast light and space movement. Also included in the museum's holdings is a unique "uncollectible" earthwork, a 1,500-foot-long groove cut into the Nevada desert.

Beneath the galleries at MOCA, the Ahmanson Auditorium presents media and live performances, and video art shows. The museum broadcasts a radio show called "The Territory of Art." A unique program, "Art Start," is geared to elementary school teachers and students to develop an understanding of contemporary art. It includes extensive teacher workshops, curriculum guides, student visits, and parent-child workshops.

Both museum gift shops sell art books, posters, contemporary jewelry and gifts, toys, movies, T-shirts, and tote bags. There is a cafe on the gallery level at MOCA, and restaurants in the Crocker Center across the street from MOCA. No eating facilities at TC. Wheelchair access at both museums.

Enter MOCA from the parking complex and take the elevator across the courtyard to the museum. There is ample parking for MOCA directly beneath the structure in the California Plaza garage and also in Lot 16 at First St. and Grand Ave. Valet parking is available at Crocker Center at its Hope St. entrance. Additional parking can be found at the Music Center Garage at 135 North Grand Ave. where DASH shuttle service picks up passengers. Fees from $4 to $12.50 per day. At TC there are parking lots near First and Central Ave. ($1.50 to $3 per day maximum) and at 140 North San Pedro ($4 maximum on weekdays and $1.50 per car evenings and weekends).

Open Tuesday, Wednesday, Saturday, and Sunday 11 A.M.–6 P.M., Thursday and Friday 11 A.M.–8 P.M. Closed Mondays, Thanksgiving, Christmas, and New Year's Day. Admission is $4 for adults, $3 for students with ID, $2 for seniors. Children under 12 and prescheduled school groups free. Free admission on Thursday 5–8 P.M. For more information call (213) 621-2766 or write to the museum at the South Grand Ave. address.

Museum of Neon Art

704 Traction Ave., Los Angeles, CA 90013

GETTING THERE: Traction Ave. runs east of Alameda St., between 2nd and 3rd streets near Little Tokyo in downtown Los Angeles. It is one mile north of the Santa Monica Fwy (I-10), one mile west of the Golden State Fwy (I-5), ½ mile south of the Hollywood Fwy (U.S. 101) and one mile east of the Harbor Fwy (I-110).

Neon art is experiencing a renaissance and MONA is the first museum in the world dedicated to preserving, documenting, and exhibiting works of neon, electric, and kinetic art. Patented in 1915, neon was originally used only for commercial signs, but today artists are rediscovering its excitement and versatility. MONA's exhibitions include works from the museum's permanent vintage and contemporary collections. Visitors will find contemporary oil paintings with neon illumination, assemblages of found objects given the illusion of motion by tubes of moving neon, and contemporary designs mounted in the traditional sign style with neon tubing or masses of colored light bulbs. The vintage collection includes signs from the twenties through the sixties. Another recent addition to neon design is the use of computers, which allow innovative animation with endless possibilities.

MONA's founder, neon artist Lili Lakich, wants to preserve these rarely seen works, and to exhibit and encourage artists exploring this medium. Since MONA intends to find a larger facility in which to house its growing exhibitions and resources, call ahead to be sure of its current location. The gift shop sells books on neon history, design, and techniques; video cassettes; posters; and neon gifts such as clocks, orbit lamps, bottled lightning, neon Buddhas, handblown eight-foot zigzags, and encased neon sculptures. Guest lectures. No restaurants. Street parking. Wheelchair access.

Open Tuesday–Saturday 11 A.M.–6 P.M. Admission is $2.50 for adults, children under 16 free. For more information call (213) 617-1580.

Natural History Museum of Los Angeles County

900 Exposition Blvd., Los Angeles, CA 90007

GETTING THERE: From the Santa Monica Fwy (I-10) take the Vermont Ave. exit south to Exposition Blvd. Turn left. From Harbor Fwy (I-110), take the Exposition Blvd. exit west to Menlo St.

Opened in 1913, this is the third largest natural history museum in the nation. It houses over 15 million artifacts and specimens which cover more than 300 million years of the earth's history. Visitors can instantly see why this is the most often visited museum in California. Over twenty-six galleries are devoted to American and California history, gems and minerals, marine biology, anthropology, archaeology, paleontology, ornithology, botany, entomology, herpetology, zoology, mammalogy, marine zoology, and industrial, military, and transportation technology. There are fine exhibitions of vertebrate fossils, minerals, fish, mammals, butterflies, American history artifacts, and North American Indian, pre-Columbian and African materials, as well as costumes and textiles. Other galleries display collections of birds and eggs, and the dinosaur collections are especially popular. There is also an unexpected collection of five hundred works of art, including paintings by Edwin Deaken, Lemuel Wiles, and Theodore Wores; drawings and prints by Currier and Ives and John James Audubon; and two hundred fine Navajo rugs.

One of the most beautiful galleries highlights lifelike scenes of North American, African, and exotic mammals. Other exhibits include one of the largest fish collections, the largest southwestern moth and butterfly collection, and the largest ant collection in the country. The darkened Gem and Mineral Hall dramatically displays some of the museum's 2,000 specimens including California's state gemstone. In the Growth of the Nation Hall there is a cross-section of a prairie schooner, a depiction of colonial period rooms and historic settings, and a bell cast by Paul Revere in 1811.

Three gift shops offer an abundance of museum-related items. The bookshop has an extensive selection of books and records. The Dinosaur Shop sells a large selection of dinosaur items (even a dinosaur teapot!) from 28¢ to $100. The Ethnic Art Shop offers an array of jewelry, textiles, apparel, pottery, rugs, dolls, masks, and

A detailed display at the Natural History Museum of Los Angeles County. Courtesy of museum.

baskets. There is a museum cafeteria and a McDonald's in the park. Free visitor parking is limited but there is a $1 parking lot off Menlo Street as well. Bring four quarters.

Open year-round, Tuesday–Sunday 10 A.M.–5 P.M. 9 A.M.–6 P.M. on weekends from April to September. Admission is $3 for adults, $1.50 for seniors and students, 75¢ for children 5–12, children under 5 free. Also free the first Tuesday of each month. For the recorded message call (213) 744-3466 and for more information call (213) 744-3414.

John Rowland Historic Home
16021 East Gale Ave., La Puente, CA 91745

GETTING THERE: Go east on the Pomona Fwy (60). Exit at Hacienda Blvd., which is east of the San Gabriel River Fwy (I–605), and go north to Gale Ave. Turn right and go two blocks to a bus parking lot. Turn and follow a narrow dirt road to the house.

John Rowland was the partner of William Workman in leading the first overland expedition of settlers to southern California in 1841. (See Workman and Temple Homestead.) The partners owned a store in Taos, New Mexico, but built the family homes near one another to the east of Los Angeles in what is now called La Puente. Furnishings of the home are from 1855 to 1920.

Wisteria planted on three sides of the house in 1920 provides a beautiful setting for the home's springtime Wisteria Tea, and the October barbecue is served beneath its woodsy climbing vine. The home's living museum demonstrates soap making, stenciling, butter making, weaving, spinning, and clothes washing. These demonstrations are a treat for children and adults to watch.

At Christmas the rooms are decorated with Victorian themes. Delightful demonstrations are given of Christmas holiday traditions from 1855 to 1920. Special tours are provided for school groups. Picnic area, no eating facilities. No wheelchair access. Free parking.

Open every Wednesday and the first Sunday of each month, 1–4 P.M. Admission is 50¢ for adults, children free. For more information call (818) 336-7644 for a recorded message. Otherwise call (818) 336-2382 or (818) 336-3384.

Skirball Museum of the Hebrew Union College
3077 University Mall, Los Angeles, CA 90007

GETTING THERE: From the Harbor Fwy (I–110), exit at Exposition Blvd. and go west to Figueroa St. Turn right. Go north to 32nd St. Turn left on 32nd, and go to Hoover. Turn right, then a quick right again into the parking lot. The museum is located directly across from the University Mall Village Shopping Center.

Located in the building of Hebrew Union College on the campus of the University of Southern California, this museum features Jewish history, traditions, and ceremonial art.

A "Walk Through the Past" presents a permanent display of archaeological findings from the ancient Near East, and from a *tell*, a hill-like structure formed over generations by the accumulation of layer upon layer of cultural material. When archaeologists examined the findings of the tell, gently peeling away each layer, it was like "turning the pages of history." Photos of archaeologists at such a site accompany the recreation of the tell.

Jewish traditions are depicted through displays of various ceremonial objects used during religious rites of birth, adolescence, marriage, and death. Beautiful menorahs, sedar plates, and spice boxes used in the celebrations of the Holy Days reflect the rich heritage of customs and religious art.

The "Realm of Torah" houses the Torah and its protective cases, mantels, and finials. A unique piece is a seventeenth-century Chinese Torah case from a Chinese-Jewish community which resulted after Jewish silk traders from Persia settled in China. The museum has magnificent contemporary art shows such as "A 25–Year Retrospective of Moshe Zabari's Ceremonial Art," displaying symbolic and interpretive designs in silver. Permanent collections include Jewish ceremonial art, archaeological artifacts, textiles, decorative arts, manuscripts, photos, engravings, paintings, prints, drawings, and graphics.

Tours given Sundays at 1 P.M. Reservations required for groups. The gift shop offers adult and children's books, museum publications, art objects, jewelry, fiber art, posters, note cards, and Judaic religious artifacts. No restaurant. Wheelchair access.

Open Tuesday–Friday 11 A.M.–4 P.M., Sunday 10 A.M.–5 P.M. Free admission and parking. For more information and to reserve tours, call (213) 749-3424.

Southwest Museum and Casa de Adobe
234 Museum Dr., Los Angeles, CA 90042

GETTING THERE: Exit the Pasadena Fwy (I–110) at Avenue 43 and follow signs to the corner of Museum Drive and Marmion. The museum and adobe are located within two blocks of the Lummis Home and Heritage Square. The parking lot is up the long driveway, but if visitors park on the street they will enjoy the additional pleasure of entering the museum by way of the long tunnel set with dioramas depicting Indian life.

Set on a hill overlooking the Highland Park area, the beautiful two-story mission-style Southwest Museum is the only major museum in southern California solely devoted to Native American culture. Spacious exhibition halls display only a portion of the holdings of early California Indian art and artifacts. In one wing an elaborate exhibition includes a full-size Pomo acorn granary, a petroglyph, or rock art facsimile, and a recreated eighteen-foot tepee. The museum's basket collection is one of the largest in the country, and its extensive pottery collection shows a great diversity of design. It also contains an outstanding collection of Kachinas.

Changing major exhibitions have celebrated contemporary art by Native American women, contemporary sculpture, lithographs by Mexican artists, an elaborate display of Northwest Coast Indian Art, and a show highlighting eight contemporary Indian artists. The museum's permanent collection includes 500,000 objects of Southwest art, Hispanic pieces, photography, decorative folk art, artifacts of the Spanish-Colonial and Mexican eras, and objects from prehistoric and historic North, Central, and South America. Self-guided tours with the aid of brochure.

Casa de Adobe
4605 North Figueroa, Los Angeles, CA 90042

A few blocks from the Southwest Museum is Casa de Adobe, a reconstruction of a pre–1850s Spanish California rancho. Two rooms are furnished with objects contemporary to the period. The museum hosts films, lectures, workshops, and seminars on Native

Hopi Kachina doll, representing fertility. Made of cottonwood, feathers, and horse-hair. Courtesy of Southwest Museum. Photo by Donald Meyer.

American and Hispanic culture and history. It also holds a family Christmas party each year and a festival of Native American arts during October.

The museum's Braun Research Library houses 200,000 items including 50,000 books, 500 manuscripts, and hundreds of sound-recordings and tapes and attracts scholars worldwide. The museum has a 250-seat auditorium.

The gift shop has a diverse array of Native American and Hispanic art, posters, pictures, crafts, jewelry, and books. A picnic area is located in the historic Sycamore Grove Park directly across from Casa de Adobe. Wheelchair access. Free parking.

Open Tuesday–Sunday 11 A.M.–5 P.M. Admission is $3 for adults, $1.50 for senior citizens and students, $1 for children 7–18, under 7 free. For more information call (213) 221-2164. For the adobe, call (213) 225-8653.

Wells Fargo History Museum

33 South Grand Ave. (Crocker Plaza), Los Angeles, CA 90071

GETTING THERE: Take Hollywood Fwy (U.S. 101) to the Temple St. exit. Follow Hope past the Music Center and turn left after First St. Turn right and continue on Hope to the Crocker Plaza Building. Turn left to park inside Crocker Plaza. The history museum is across the street from the Museum of Contemporary Art.

In 1882 Henry Wells and William G. Fargo, two eastern business-men who had watched the Gold Rush phenomenon and recognized its potential for an express post and banking business, opened their first office in San Francisco. This beautiful small museum explains that beginning and the company's expansion.

The visitor finds interesting lifelike displays, such as a Wells Fargo office typical of Gold Rush Express offices of the 1850s, where visitors may listen to a typical day in the life of a Wells Fargo Express agent. The full-size replica of a nineteenth-century Concord stagecoach is well worth seeing. Mark Twain called the Concord stagecoach "a cradle on wheels," and it is still Wells Fargo's corporate symbol.

The exhibits follow the growth of the company from banking services during the Gold Rush through stage coaching, the Pony Express, railroad, steamer lines, and, finally, in international expansion. Collections include 1,000 historic artifacts from more than 130 years of Wells Fargo history, gold quartz and gold nugget collection, and documentation and artifacts pertaining to the history of Wells Fargo and early California.

Guided tours for all age groups. The General Store gift shop has gifts pertaining to the American West, including model stage coaches, posters, agent badges, and books. Enter the parking lot on Hope Street, across from the Security Pacific National Bank building (museum parking is not validated) or park below the Museum of Contemporary Art. Several restaurants within the Crocker Plaza Building.

Open Monday–Friday 9 A.M.–4 P.M. Closed on federal holidays. Free admission. For more information and to reserve tours call (213) 253-7166.

Whittier Historical Museum
6755 Newlin Ave., Whittier, CA 90601–4019

GETTING THERE: The nearest major cross-streets to the museum are Whittier Blvd. and Pickering Ave., off the San Gabriel River Fwy (I–605). The museum is one block east of Pickering at Newlin Ave. and Philadelphia St.

Over 800 members of the Whittier Historical Society are responsible for the conversion of an old telephone company building into an interesting local history museum. Visitors enter a charming, authentically reproduced Main Street bedecked with quaint shop windows full of artifacts and antique clothes, a newspaper office, and barn replica. There is also a Quaker meeting house under construction, and an early transportation exhibit. The elegant archives room upstairs has one hundred years of Whittier history in newspaper and photography displays. The large gallery upstairs is for annual shows. The gift shop sells folk art, postcards, prints, stationery, and time capsules to fill. Restaurant across street. Wheelchair access. Free parking.

Open Saturday and Sunday 1–4 P.M. Admission is $1 for adults, 25¢ for children. For more information call (213) 945-3871.

Citrus farm exhibit. Courtesy Whittier Museum. Photo by Paul G. Thatcher.

Whittier Narrows Museum and Wildlife Sanctuary
1000 North Durfee Ave., South El Monte, CA 91734

GETTING THERE: The center is just west of the intersection of the Pomona Fwy (60) and the San Gabriel River Fwy (I-605).

Located in a 277-acre refuge, this museum explains the ecosystem of the San Gabriel Valley and has a one-mile, self-guided nature trail. Birds, reptiles, amphibians (both alive and preserved) of the riparian community are on display, and ecological exhibits explain the San Gabriel River and the adjacent vicinity. A rehabilitation area provides care for animals prior to their release back into the wild.

The center has numerous special programs of lectures, workshops, hands-on exhibits, and scheduled bird walks on weekends. Two major annual events are the Spring Open House and a Christmas Boutique that sells nature gifts and native plants. Guided tours by naturalists are available for school groups. Also has library and nursery of plants native to the streamside environment. The nearest picnic area is ¼ mile away at Legg Lake. Wheelchair access to museum and to a portion of the nature trail.

Open daily 9 A.M.–5 P.M. Free admission and parking. For more information call (818) 444-1872.

Workman and Temple Homestead
15415 East Don Julian Road, City of Industry, CA 91744

GETTING THERE: The museum is located twenty miles east of downtown Los Angeles. Take the Pomona Fwy (60) east and exit north on the Hacienda Blvd. exit. Go one mile north to Don Julian Road.

Representative of 1840s, 1870s, and 1920s home furnishings and daily life, the Workman and Temple Homestead is a six-acre landmark composed of eight structures documenting nearly 140 years of southern California middle-class life. Included among the structures are the Workman House, an 1840s adobe which was remodeled into a manor house in the 1870s; a water tower and pump house, circa 1872; a Greek Revival mausoleum, built in 1919; a Spanish Colonial Revival residence and its adjoining tepee-like

Courtyard and fountain, La Casa Nueva at Workman and Temple Homestead.
Photo by Julius Shulman.

retreat, both built in the 1920s; a contemporary *glorieta*, or gazebo, and the Pio Pico Gallery visitors center.

The homestead was once the property of William Workman who, with John Rowland, led the first overland expedition of settlers to southern California in 1841. Workman and his wife had local Indians build an adobe residence on their rancho and it grew from a simple structure in 1843 to a larger home by 1872. In the 1870s the Workman family became sufficiently wealthy to remodel the adobe into an English manor house. In 1917, Workman's grandson, Walter P. Temple, Sr., began to restore the homestead and built the primary residence, La Casa Nueva, a Spanish-Colonial mansion. Displays of fine decorative arts inside La Casa Nueva represent the life-style of an upper-middle class California family in the 1920s.

Special programs include films, lectures, workshops, concerts, cooking, and craft classes. Special group tours are provided for the mentally or physically disabled, senior citizens, and school groups. A special school program, "A Journey Through Time," has been created for fourth graders in the local school districts. Nonprofit arts and education groups may hold special events on the Homestead grounds for a fee. Contact the office.

Annual events include a Christmas Open House with entertainment and refreshments. Each May the museum recognizes National Preservation Week with a one-day architectural crafts fair. The fair includes live craft demonstrations, house tours, entertainment, and refreshments typical of the 1870s through the 1920s. Picnic area is available for group tours by reservation. Ramps, special parking, and special programs for disabled persons.

Open Tuesday–Friday 1–4 P.M., Saturday–Sunday 10 A.M.–4 P.M. Closed Mondays, major holidays and the fourth weekend of each month. Free parking and admission. For more information or to schedule a group tour call (818) 968-8492.

◆

Chapter Two

Mid-Wilshire
and West Side

Adamson House *(see Malibu Lagoon Museum)*

Angel's Attic
516 Colorado Ave., Santa Monica, CA 90401

GETTING THERE: From Santa Monica Fwy (I–10) take the 5th St. exit. The museum is in the blue Victorian house on the immediate right.

One of only a handful of toy museums in the United States, this is a must for miniature enthusiasts. "Angels" refers to the Angels for Autistic Children, a support group for the Brentwood Center for Educational Therapy. Their attic is a two-story Victorian house, built in 1895, that houses a museum of antique dollhouses, miniatures, and toys.

Saved from demolition, this vintage house is finely restored to its original beauty. Tea is served on the front porch which is elegantly furnished in white wicker, and overlooks Victorian flower beds. The front porch is also the vantage point for viewing the startling contrast of this ornate period house reflected perfectly in the contemporary glass building across the street. Inside the museum approximately forty dollhouses and other miniatures are on display including visiting exhibits from other collections. From Christmas through February, Santa's Workshop, with a fully furnished dormitory for his elves, depicts every detail of Christmas holiday preparation. The Gentleman's Gallery has miniature tools with hand-carved handles and handwrought blades and an assortment of antique banks, wind-up tin toys, and an LBG electric train.

A pleasant site for afternoon tea. Courtesy Angel's Attic.

Victorian American dollhouse. Courtesy Angel's attic.

Metered street parking only. Requests for tours must be made in writing to special tours coordinator. The gift shop offers a small assortment of fine, handcrafted miniature figures, furniture, and accessories. Tea is served to museum visitors for $2.50. Special parking behind the house. Wheelchair access.

Open Thursday–Sunday 12:30–4:30 P.M. Admission is $3 for adults, $1 for children under 12, $2 for senior citizens. For more information call (213) 394–8331.

Craft and Folk Art Museum
5814 Wilshire Blvd., Los Angeles, CA 90036

GETTING THERE: From the Santa Monica Fwy (I–10), take the Fairfax Ave. exit north to Wilshire Blvd. and turn right. Look for the museum's long entrance awning, located across from the Page Museum and the La Brea tar pits.

Concentrating on folk art from around the world as well as contemporary design and architecture, this museum is known for its lively, colorful exhibitions. Using video, musical and live demonstrations to produce up to six major shows each year, the Craft and Folk Art Museum strives to celebrate ethnic diversity and promote interest in contemporary crafts and artisans. The museum offers a variety of special programs to coincide with ethnic festivities in the community. In recent years these have included the American-Korean Centennial Celebration, "Japan Today," and "Egypt Today." The museum's Mask Festival has become a very popular event and is held biannually. They offer mask-making workshops, and the program culminates in a Mask Parade along Wilshire Boulevard.

The museum's permanent collection largely comprises Japanese and Mexican folk art collections, East Indian quilts, masks, and native textiles, and contemporary crafts. In addition to its fine exhibitions and festivals, the museum has attained prominence for its educational programs of lectures and workshops in craft, design, and folklore. Educational services include conferences, docent tours, studio demonstrations, and symposia. A scheduled Sunday Family Night offers storytelling and a craft activity. Families may bring their own picnic supper. Reservations are required. The museum also hosts school tours and The Movable Museum, an outreach program that provides classroom workshops led by local artists and artisans for fourth and fifth graders.

Docent tours are conducted on Saturdays at 1 P.M. in the main gallery. For group tours call (213) 934-3082. The museum also houses an artists' slide registry that is open by appointment. For information call (213) 934-7239. Visitors are invited to browse at the museum gift shop, known for its broad range of folk art and unique contemporary gifts and jewelry, as well as a large selection of books on international folk crafts. A restaurant and additional gallery are located upstairs. The Egg and the Eye is open for lunch daily except Monday 11 A.M.–3 P.M. Brunch is served on Saturday and Sunday 10 A.M.–3 P.M. Reservations are recommended. Street parking is limited, but museum parking is available at hourly rates. Wheelchair access on street level only.

Museum open Tuesday–Sunday 11 A.M.–5 P.M. Closed Mondays. Admission for adults is $1.50, 75¢ for children 12 and under, $1 for senior citizens and students with ID. For more information call (213) 937-5544.

Donald Douglas Museum and Library
2800 Perimeter Road, Santa Monica, CA 90405

GETTING THERE: From the Santa Monica Fwy (I–10) east, take the Bundy Dr. exit and go south. From the San Diego Fwy (I–405) follow it to the Santa Monica Fwy west and exit at Bundy Dr. Go south toward the airport. The museum is located on the north side of the Santa Monica Airport.

The Donald Douglas Museum and Library depicts the history of the Douglas Aircraft Company with murals, models, and photographs. Douglas aircraft flown in World War II, Korea, and Vietnam are featured. There are approximately fifteen aircraft in the museum and seven outside. Other large exhibits include the three-quarter-scale replica of the *Spirit of St. Louis* and the full-scale model of the Mercury space capsule, *Friendship 7*. The engine collection includes an early Lycoming, Curtiss OX5, Allison, Comet, and a 3½ HP Continental, along with full-scale models of other famous aircraft.

Smaller scale exhibits show numerous fine examples of model-makers' art. Photos of scale model airplanes from 1913 to 1945, personal items from Douglas's collection, portraits of aerospace notables, murals of scaled renditions of aircraft from 1903 to 1945, and a collection of model airplanes will interest aeronautic enthusiasts. The library houses engineering drawings, aerospace books, aviation and space fiction and nonfiction, prints, photos, and films. The library walls display prints, awards, and aviation memorabilia. Open to the public, it includes a large area for reference study.

Special programs include classes in making models from scratch or kits. There is also a model shop for advanced modelmakers. The gift shop offers aerospace models, 100 lithographs, and unique jewelry. Restaurant in the building and wheelchair access.

Open weekdays only, noon–5 P.M. Closed on most major holidays. A $2 donation is requested. For more information call (213) 390-3339.

J. Paul Getty Art Museum
17985 Pacific Coast Hwy, Malibu, CA 90265

GETTING THERE: From the San Fernando Valley, take Topanga Canyon Blvd. west to Pacific Coast Hwy and turn south. The museum is between Topanga Canyon Blvd. and Sunset Blvd. Coming from Santa Monica, the Santa Monica Fwy (I–10) merges into the Pacific Coast Hwy.

Visiting the Getty for the first time is a remarkable experience. The magnificent building is a replica of the Villa dei Papiri, a 100 A.D. Roman villa overlooking the Bay of Naples. The mountainside setting, formal gardens, and ocean view are spectacular. In addition, the museum's gardens are graced with trees, flowers, and herbs that would have belonged in the setting of the Villa dei Papiri two thousand years ago. Visitors always stop to admire the exquisite grounds, the long narrow reflecting pool, and bronze statuary before stepping inside to view the magnificent collections.

The museum's permanent collections center on seven areas: Greek and Roman antiquities, pre-twentieth-century Western European paintings, drawings, decorative arts, sculpture, illuminated manuscripts, and nineteenth- and twentieth-century European and American photographs.

The J. Paul Getty Museum replicates a 100 A.D. Roman villa. Photo by Julius Shulman.

Greek and Roman antiquities from 2500 B.C. to 300 A.D. include marble and bronze sculptures, mosaics, vases, and objects in other media. On the upper level the decorative arts galleries and paneled period rooms display one of the finest collections of eighteenth-century French decorative arts in the United States, including furniture, carpets, tapestries, chandeliers, clocks, gilt and bronze pieces, porcelains and cloisonne enamels, and ceramics and glass.

All major schools of western painting from the early fourteenth to the late nineteenth century are represented. Visitors may see works by Masaccio, Bouts, David, Mantegna, Rembrandt, Rubens, La Tour, Millet, Van Dyck, Boucher, and Gainsborough and master drawings by Raphael, Dürer, Bernini, Rubens, Ingres, Goya, Watteau, Cezanne, van Gogh, and Millet. The European and American photography collection, from the 1840s to the 1950s, presents the work of Cameron, Talbot, Nadar, Weston, Man Ray, and others. Spanning the period from the Middle Ages to the end of the nineteenth century, the sculpture collection has works by Cellini, Giambologna, Goffini, de Vries, Tacca, Verhulst, Houdon, Clodion, Barye, and Carpeaux. A collection of illuminated manuscripts from the ninth through seventeenth centuries is dramatically displayed in darkened galleries.

All the collections except the antiquities will be moved to the museum in the new J. Paul Getty Center in Brentwood planned for completion in 1993. Designed by Los Angeles architect, Richard Meier and partners, the Center will be a state-of-the-art facility for art exhibition, education, and conservation. The Malibu site will then be the only American museum exclusively devoted to Greek and Roman antiquities.

Special programs include lectures, concerts, and daily gallery talks. The schedule is posted near the information desk. At the entrance to the main garden docents offer introductory talks every fifteen minutes, 9:45 A.M.–3 P.M. Also available inside are an illustrated *Handbook of the Collections* and a helpful brochure.

Educational services include gallery programs for school groups and for adult groups affiliated with art or academic institutions. Thursday evening lecture series. For information and reservations, call (213) 458-2003.

Scholarly art books, cards, posters, slides, and art reproductions are available in the bookstore. Mail-order catalog. The Garden Tea Room offers self-service lunch 11 A.M.–2:30 P.M., desserts and beverages 9:30 A.M.–4:30 P.M. Advance parking reservations are required, as street parking is not permitted. Pedestrians are not admitted, except for those arriving by taxi, bicycle, motorcycle, or public bus. Bus passengers must present a museum pass, available for no additional charge from the driver. These restrictions prevent congestion in the adjacent residential area. Wheelchair access.

Open year-round, Tuesday–Saturday 10 A.M.–5 P.M. Closed Mondays, New Year's Day, Fourth of July, Thanksgiving and Christmas. Admission is free. For more information call (213) 458-2003.

Los Angeles County Museum of Art (LACMA)
5905 Wilshire Blvd., Los Angeles, CA 90036

GETTING THERE: Take the Santa Monica Fwy (I–10) to the La Brea exit and go north to Wilshire Blvd. Turn left.

This vast museum complex, with its fifty-foot entranceway, massive columns, walkways, and pitched skylights includes the Ahmanson Gallery, the Anderson Building, the Leo S. Bing Center, the Frances and Armand Hammer Wing, the B. G. Cantor Sculpture Garden, and the Times Mirror Central Courtyard. In addition to these well-known galleries and their holdings, the Pavilion of Japanese Art is projected to open in the summer of 1988. Housing the Shinenkan collection, it will become the finest collection of Edo period (1616–1868) paintings and scrolls in the western world. The permanent and visiting exhibitions compel many museum-goers to visit the complex many times a year. All current exhibits are posted in each building. The museum's permanent collections represent the full scope of western art history from Egyptian and Greco-Roman sculpture and antiquities; Asian painting, sculpture, and ceramics; pre-Columbian art; European and American painting, sculpture, prints, drawings, and decorative arts; Italian mosaics; twentieth-century art; costumes and textiles from around the world, including forty-nine striking American and European quilts; Asian jade and metalwork; English silver, and an antique glass collection. The Indian and Islamic art collection is considered to be one of the three most important in the world.

Special programs include an international feature film series on weekends and music concert series. For film information call (213) 857-6201. Programs for members include art and photography classes, workshops, lectures by distinguished speakers, and travel opportunities. The museum also has an art rental service. Tours available. Fifteen-minute spotlight talks on one artist or work of art are given daily at 12:30 P.M. Guided tours offered to school groups grades 4–12. Special tours for vision- and hearing-impaired visitors and senior citizens. Call the docent office at (213) 857-6109 on weekdays, 9 A.M.–4 P.M.

The museum gift shop offers a wonderful variety of art books, posters, slides, photographs, catalogs, periodicals, contemporary and ethnic jewelry, and many gifts. A cafeteria is located on the upper plaza. Wheelchair access. Wheelchairs can be obtained at no extra charge. No strollers allowed during crowded special exhibits.

Open Tuesday–Friday 10 A.M.–5 P.M., Saturday and Sunday 10 A.M.–6 P.M. Admission is $1.50, 75¢ for students with ID, senior citizens over 62, and visitors under 17. The second Tuesday of each month is free to everyone. Joint admission with the George C. Page is $6 for adults, $4.75 for students and seniors, and $2.25 for children. For more information call (213) 857-6111 for a recorded message. For information for the hearing impaired, call (213) 857–0098.

Malibu Lagoon Museum/Adamson House
23200 Pacific Coast Hwy, Malibu, CA 90265

GETTING THERE: Take the Pacific Coast Hwy to 23200, 300 yards north of the Malibu Pier.

Nestled inconspicuously in an estate setting between the Pacific Coast Highway and the ocean, Rhoda Rindge Adamson House is an elegant 1920s Spanish-Moorish hacienda. Each of its ten furnished rooms incorporates lavish use of decorative tiles from the once internationally famous Malibu Potteries. Other outstanding features of the house are handwrought filigree ironwork, molded ceilings, and hand-carved teakwood doors.

The Rindge family's Malibu ranch once encompassed all of Malibu. Visitors can also see a rare collection of artifacts from the Chumash Indians who once were a large Malibu population. An exhibit of the tile patterns and tiles produced at Malibu Potteries and an explanation of the various steps involved in their production is fascinating. Behind the museum is a humorous memento of the family that once lived here—a large, colorfully tiled outdoor bathtub for the Adamsons' golden retrievers.

Tour reservations are required only for groups of ten or more. Call (213) 456-8432. The gift shop offers a modest assortment of books, stationery, and gifts. There are no eating facilities at the museum. Street parking is limited. Parking is $3 per car at the nearby county lot. Wheelchair access only on first floor of house and into museum.

Open Wednesday–Saturday 10 A.M.–1:30 P.M. Admission is free. For more information call (213) 456-8432.

Martyrs Memorial and Museum of the Holocaust
6505 Wilshire Blvd., Los Angeles, CA 90048

GETTING THERE: From the Santa Monica Fwy (I-10), exit at Fairfax or La Cienega and go north. The museum is located on Wilshire Blvd., between these avenues, in the Jewish community building. In Fall 1988, the museum will be located at 6501 Wilshire Blvd.

This memorial museum is a place for remembrance of the Holocaust. A historic chronicle, encompassing the rise of the Third Reich, the relocation of Jews to ghettos, the establishment of concentration camps, and the tragic death of six million adults and children is portrayed in photographs and documents of the S.S. and other Nazi institutions. Visitors who want to be informed about daily life in the death camps, the Resistance movement, the liberation, and the aftermath of fascism can view the museum's audio-visual exhibits that include the Eichmann trial and taped eyewitness accounts of camp survivors.

A special collection of displays and detailed drawings by Leo Haas, woodcuts, paintings, and watercolors of life in the ghettos and camps are also on view. The exhibit includes poems and sculpture by concentration camp prisoners. Next to the museum exhibition hall is the Martyrs' Memorial Chapel, a place for meditation and prayer. Educational services include lecture series, teacher training, workshops, exhibitions, and resource materials such as films, videos, books, and curricula. The museum is an annual sponsor of citywide Yom Hashoah Commemoration Ceremony, or Holocaust Remembrance Day. A special program of films, lectures, and workshops is offered regularly. Parking garage. Tours are available for individuals, but reservations are required for groups. Call (213) 651-3175. Coffee shop. Wheelchair access.

Open Monday–Thursday 9 A.M.–4:45 P.M., Friday 9 A.M.–3 P.M., and Sunday 1–5 P.M. Closed Saturdays. Free admission. For more information call (213) 651-3175.

George C. Page Museum of La Brea Discoveries
5801 Wilshire Blvd., Los Angeles, CA 90036

GETTING THERE: From the Santa Monica Fwy (I-10), take the La Brea Ave. exit, and go north to Wilshire. Turn left. From the Hollywood Fwy (101), take the Santa Monica Blvd. exit, turn west to Fairfax, then left to Wilshire Blvd. It is located next to the Los Angeles County Museum of Art.

The George C. Page Museum (part of the Los Angeles County Museum of Natural History) is a paleontology museum built to house over one million Ice Age mammals, plants, and birds recovered from the Rancho La Brea tar pits in next-door Hancock Park.

The pits were dug after the Civil War for commercial use for asphalt in paving streets, greasing wheels, caulking ships, patching houses, and sealing roofs. In 1916 the land was donated to the county as a park by G. Allen Hancock, and in 1977 the museum was built by philanthropist George C. Page and given to the county. The beautiful building, with its stone relief of prehistoric animals and plants, includes an atrium garden, and sits near the Lake Pit where visitors can view full-size replicas of animals in the tar. Other pits are located in Hancock Park between the museum and the art museum. Be sure to see the current pit excavation of a twenty-eight-foot square pit, then watch the work in progress inside the museum through the glass-walled paleontology laboratory. In no other major southern California museum can visitors view this living demonstration of collecting, preparing, and cataloging a scientific collection.

Featuring over thirty major exhibitions, the museum displays mounted skeletons of mammoths, sabertooth cats, wolves, and birds. One fascinating exhibit is the "La Brea Woman" who, due to

A dramatic story of entrapment in the LaBrea tar pits unfolds at the George C. Page Museum of La Brea Discoveries. Courtesy of museum.

technological special effects, changes from a skeleton to a complete, fleshed-out figure during the brief time the visitor looks at
her. Holdings of over 1.5 million specimens include 500,000 fossil
bones, the largest collection in the U.S. These include the lower
jaw of a rare American lion believed to be over 38,000 years old,
plus bones from rare, dwarf pronghorned antelopes.

The museum is designed for self-guided tours, the outside area can
be explored with a map guide. Public tours of the pits on Thursday
and Sunday at 1 P.M., and of the museum Tuesday and Sunday at
2 P.M. and at 11:30 A.M. on weekends. Reservations for groups
required. Docent-guided tours for school groups can be arranged.
All group tours call (213) 857–6306 Wednesday–Friday after 1 P.M.
The Museum Shop offers an assortment of books, posters, educational aids, toys, and gift items relating to paleontology. Public
cafeteria at art museum. No formal picnic facilities, but lawns surround the museum. Free parking in the Hancock Park parking lot,
also street parking. Wheelchair access.

Open Tuesday–Sunday 10 A.M.–5 P.M. Closed Mondays, Thanksgiving, Christmas,
and New Year's Day. Admission is $3 for adults, $1.50 for students and senior citizens, and 75¢ for children 5 to 12. Children under 5 are free, and the second
Tuesday of every month is free for everyone. A combined ticket with same-day
entrance to Page Museum and Los Angeles County Museum of Art is $4.50 for
adults, $2.25 for students and seniors, and $1 for children.

Santa Monica Heritage Museum
2612 Main St., Santa Monica, CA 90405

GETTING THERE: Going west on Santa Monica Fwy (I-10), take
the 4th St. and 5th St. exit. Go straight off off-ramp to 4th St. Go
south on 4th to Pico Blvd. Turn right (west), then left on Main. Go
about four blocks to the museum.

This local history museum is housed in a vintage home that was
originally built on Ocean Avenue. Only after the house was moved
to its present site did the research reveal that it had been built by
Senator John Percival Jones in 1894.

Room furnishings reflect different periods of Santa Monica's development from the 1890s and early 1900s. The kitchen is a copy of
Merle Norman's 1920s kitchen where her cosmetics business
began. An upstairs gallery features contemporary art,

Santa Monica Heritage Museum shares local history. Photo by Sara LeBien.

photography, quilt and pottery shows, and empire-period fashions. Lectures, seminars, and concerts are also held here. Summer outdoor concerts are held as well as a Christmas toy show with annual themes.

Lectures pertaining to current exhibitions and practical workshops on subjects such as the care and storage of photos are scheduled regularly. Free parking. Guided tours for all visitors. Reservations required two weeks in advance for groups. Restaurant nearby in another restored historic building. A gift shop in the front parlor offers an assortment of Santa Monica history books and reproductions of Victorian children's books. Wheelchair access.

Open Sunday noon–4 P.M., Thursday–Saturday 11 A.M.–4 P.M. Admission is free. For more information call (213) 397-8537.

UCLA Museum of Cultural History
Haines Hall, University of California at Los Angeles, Los Angeles, CA 90024

GETTING THERE: Exit the San Diego Fwy (I–405) at Sunset Blvd. Go east on Sunset to the UCLA campus. Purchase a parking token ($3) from a parking information booth, and get further directions. The museum is located in Haines Hall on the northern part of the campus, adjacent to Royce Hall, within easy walking distance to the Sculpture Garden and Wight Gallery complex.

The exhibitions in the gallery at the UCLA Museum of Cultural History always have great visual impact on the visitor, from New Guinea masks to Mexican folk art, to shadow puppets from India and Bali. The museum has a prestigious African art collection and an extensive array of Central and South American textiles. There are new exhibitions every eight weeks.

The museum was originally established in 1973 as a repository for UCLA's ethnographic collections, but with the vision of its founder, former university chancellor Franklin E. Murphy, and the guidance and expertise of the late Ralph Altman, the museum has gained international prominence for the quality of its collections, publications, programs, and exhibitions. It is ranked among the top four university museums of ethnography and archaeology in the U.S. Collections comprise 50,000 objects representing

Haida mask from British Columbia. Courtesy UCLA Museum of Cultural History. Gift of the Wellcome Trust. Photo by Richard Todd.

The Haines Gallery at the UCLA Museum of Cultural History. Courtesy of museum. Photo by Richard Todd.

contemporary and traditional cultures of Africa, Oceania, Latin and Native America, Asia, and Europe, including 15,000 textiles. The pre-Columbian art collection is outstanding. Be sure to walk the corridors of Haines Hall to view the additional displays in the hall cases. A new facility, the Fowler Museum of Cultural History, is being built near Royce Hall and is due to open in Fall 1989. This impressive structure will devote 20,000 square feet to exhibition space and host up to eight major shows each year. Pre-exhibition festivities such as arts demonstrations, music, and dance will frequently open each show.

The museum offers educational materials and programs for teachers and schools and also tours, lectures, and special programs for the public. There is also an active publication program of catalogs, monographs, educational filmstrips, cards, and posters.

The Haines Gallery presently sells exhibition catalogs. The new museum shop will sell books, catalogs, jewelry, folk art, and other museum gifts. Reservations required for tours. Parking tokens may be purchased at the parking information booth. Special parking, ramps, and wheelchair access.

The Haines Hall facility is open Wednesday–Sunday noon–5 P.M. Closed on major holidays and school holidays. Admission is free. For more information on the museum's scheduled exhibitions, as well as lectures, workshops, and receptions call (213) 825-4361.

UCLA Wight Gallery Complex
405 Hilgard Ave. (UCLA campus), Los Angeles, CA 90024

Franklin D. Murphy Sculpture Garden
Grunwald Center
Wight Art Gallery

GETTING THERE: From the San Diego Fwy (I–405), take the Sunset Blvd. exit and follow Sunset east to Hilgard Ave. Turn right onto the UCLA campus and stop at the nearest information booth for parking instructions. Parking tokens are $3. From the south side of the UCLA campus, take Wilshire Blvd. to Hilgard and turn left onto the campus.

The art complex on the University of California campus in Los Angeles includes three distinct exhibition areas. Visible on approach is the Franklin D. Murphy Sculpture Garden, a spacious five-acre lawn on the north side of campus near the Fine Arts and Theater Arts buildings. Named for its founder and former university chancellor, Franklin D. Murphy, the sculpture garden is the setting for seventy pieces of modern sculpture by distinguished artists such as Hans Arp, Francisco Zuniga, Eric Gill, Robert Graham, Barbara Hepworth, Jacques Lipchitz, Henri Matisse, Jóan Miró, Henry Moore, George Rickey, Auguste Rodin, Richard Smith, Louis H. Sullivan, and Peter Voulkos. Docent-led tours are a must for the visitor interested in learning about this fine collection.

Beyond the garden is the Wight Art Gallery, dedicated to the original gallery director and former chairman of the art department. One of the gallery's main accomplishments has been to provide exhibits that meet the needs of the academic community as well as the general public. In an exhibition space of 14,000 square feet, novel multimedia shows have celebrated the works of contemporary German artists, nineteenth-century Italian painters, American impressionists, paintings by American women, and a retrospective of Henri Matisse. The gallery also houses the UCLA Museum of Cultural History's annual show, a major exhibition.

On the upper level of the Wight Gallery, the Grunwald Center contains approximately 30,000 prints, photographs, drawings, and illustrated books representing the thirteenth through twentieth centuries. Important works in the print collection include numerous Old Master prints and drawings, the Frank Lloyd Wright Collection of Japanese Prints, the Fred Grunwald Collection of Daumier Prints, the Tamarind Lithography Archives, works of French impressionists and German expressionists, nineteenth- and twentieth-century American illustration, and European costume design and ornament prints. The Grunwald Center is open to the public during scheduled exhibitions by appointment.

Special programs and educational services at the art complex include films, lectures, workshops, and an art library. The UCLA Art Council and the Friends of the Graphic Arts organize several special events each year and welcome calls for information or requests to join the mailing list. Outreach programs send announcements and educational kits to regional school districts.

Tours and lectures are offered frequently by visiting curators, docents, and other museum staff. Special tours are offered for the visually impaired. Docent tours are held daily and may be arranged in advance by calling (213) 825-3264. A good selection of exhibition catalogs, art books, cards, posters, gifts, jewelry, and folk art is available at the museum gift shop. A buffet cafeteria is located on the north side of campus with indoor and outdoor seating. Special parking, ramps, and wheelchair access.

The gallery is open to the public from September to June, and admission is free. Hours are Tuesday 11 A.M.–8 P.M., Wednesday–Friday 11 A.M.–5 P.M. Closed on major holidays. For more information call (213) 825-1461 or (213) 825-3783.

Simon Wiesenthal Center and Museum

9760 West Pico Blvd., Beverly Hills, CA 90035-4792

GETTING THERE: From the Santa Monica Fwy (I-10) take the Robertson Blvd. exit and go left on Pico Blvd. The museum is located between Beverly Blvd. and Roxbury Dr.

This museum is dedicated to revealing the struggle of human rights during the Holocaust. An exhibit of photographic collages taken primarily by Roman Vishniac, who traveled throughout Eastern Europe in the 1930s and recorded on film its final days of Jewish culture, and displays that use paintings, sculpture, videos, artifacts, photographs, scale models of the camps, and other documentation of Nazi death camps inform visitors of Jewish culture and the Holocaust. Prayer shawls, prayer books, and other artifacts found at the camps are on display.

In 1989 the exhibits will be housed in the new Beit Hashoah-Museum of Tolerance, a modern seven-level museum building complex ten times larger than the current exhibit space. The museum, built on adjoining property, will focus on the importance of protecting universal human rights and ethnic legitimacy.

Permanent collections consist of photographs of pre-Nazi European Jewry, artifacts and photographs of 1930 Eastern Europe taken from the Nazi Holocaust, memorabilia, scale models of concentration camps, paintings, and sculpture. Films and lectures. Annual events include the Holocaust Memorial Day

Commemoration. Facilities in the new complex will include a 325-seat theater, research center, media center, film and video studio, and seminar room. Educational services include an in-house training program for teaching about the Holocaust, genocide, and human rights violations. Speakers frequently serve as guest lecturers at schools and organizations. Picnic area. Free museum parking lot and street parking. Reservations required for tours. Special parking is limited. Wheelchair access.

Open Monday–Friday 9:30 A.M.–4:30 P.M., Sunday 11 A.M.–4 P.M. Closed Saturdays. Admission is free. For more information call (213) 553-9036.

Will Rogers State Historic Park
1425 Sunset Blvd., Pacific Palisades, CA 90272

GETTING THERE: From the San Diego Fwy (I–405) take Sunset Blvd. west approximately seven miles to the park entrance between Amalfi and Brooktree avenues. From the Santa Monica Fwy (I–10) take the Pacific Coast Hwy to Chautaqua Blvd. Go north to Sunset, turn right.

Originally a weekend country retreat, this house became the permanent home of Will Rogers and his family in 1928. Rogers and his capricious friends enlarged and remodeled the house so often that his son once said that whenever he came home from college he never knew where his bedroom would be. As would be expected of this warm, folksy humorist, Roger's home is a comfortable, thirty-one room rambling ranch house overlooking a rolling lawn and polo field. Believing that cowboys should never eat and sleep under the same roof, Will placed the bedrooms in an adjoining bunkhouse. The house is filled with western art and Indian objects, bronzes by Remington and Russell, Indian rugs, and quaint furniture. It has been preserved just as it was when it was a home, including the mounted steer in the living room which Will used to practice roping.

Biographical displays and a video chronicle his career from Wild West shows to vaudeville to silent films and finally, a notable career in radio and journalism. A small nature center is available for small groups by appointment. Hiking trails. Picnic area. Equestrian day is held each October. Tours available at no charge to K–12 school groups.

Will Rogers' peaceful country retreat. Photo by Sara LeBien.

Polo is usually played on Saturday 2–5 P.M. and Sunday 10 A.M.–12:30 P.M. Parking is $2 per car, $1 for seniors over 62, $20 per bus, $10 per van. Reservations must be made at least two weeks in advance for tours as well as group picnics and other events; no radios, sports, or parties allowed. Wheelchair access on the grounds and in the garage, but not into the house.

Open daily 10 A.M.–5 P.M. Closed Thanksgiving, Christmas, and New Year's Day. Admission is free. For more information on tours and polo games call (213) 454-8212.

Chapter Three

South Bay

Banning Residence Museum

P.O. Box 397, 401 East M St., Wilmington, CA 90748

GETTING THERE: From the Harbor Fwy (I–110) take the Pacific Coast Hwy exit and proceed one mile east to Avalon Blvd. Go right two blocks to M St. Turn left and continue two blocks to Banning Park.

Built in 1864, this beautiful residence was occupied by the Banning family until 1925. It is considered to be the finest extant example of nineteenth-century Greek Revival architecture in southern California. Phineas Banning was an entrepreneur whose vision and perseverance greatly influenced the early development of the Los Angeles Harbor and the communications and transportation network in California.

Three floors of richly furnished rooms show how this vibrant man and his active family lived and entertained. French Rococo Revival furniture abounds and an elaborate, carved mantel is in the living room. Other ornate adornments include a Louis XV mirror, a cut and etched gasolier, and elegant rugs and draperies. The children's rooms are full of quilts, hooked rugs, toys, and sports equipment of another era. Outside the kitchen, the old milkhouse has been restored as a one-room schoolhouse. Across the lawn the stage-coach barn houses old horse-drawn vehicles. Library facilities are available for a limited number of students.

A Victorian Christmas is held on the first Sunday of December. Films and lectures are offered to members. Tours available. Reservations necessary for ten or more. Call (213) 548-7777. School program available for grades 4–5.

An exceptionally elaborate 19th-century house. Courtesy of the Banning House.

Luncheon-Under-The-Pagoda is usually held on the first Friday of most months. Gourmet box lunches are available for touring groups of twenty or more. Bookstore and gift shop on the grounds. Picnic area is available. Free parking. Wheelchair access to grounds and barn only, special parking.

Open Tuesday–Thursday, Saturday and Sunday. Visitors are admitted at 12:30, 1:30, 2:30, and 3:30 P.M. Closed Mondays and Fridays. A $2 donation is asked of all adult visitors. Children under 12 free. For more information call (213) 548-7777.

Cabrillo Marine Museum
3720 Stephen White Dr., San Pedro, CA 90732

GETTING THERE: Take the Harbor Fwy (I–110) south to the end. Turn left on Gaffey, then left on 22nd St., right on Pacific Ave., and left at 36th St., which becomes Stephen White Dr. Continue straight ahead to where it becomes Vickery Circle Way. Go to its end.

This museum aquarium is devoted to promoting an appreciation of the marine life of southern California's coastline. Designed by architect Frank Gehry, the gray, nautical-looking building has a courtyard of colorful banners depicting the seasons of the ocean, while killer whales and hammerhead sharks float placidly above.

The exhibits inside focus on three major marine environments: rocky shores, sand and mud, and open ocean. Fascinating displays describe the plants and animals of southern California waters. Forty thousand gallons of sea water circulate through thirty-eight aquariums, outdoor tanks, and seawater laboratories. The Sandy Beach Wave Tank will delight children with a simulation of an ocean wave splashing onto plant and animal life. The Touch Tank outside allows visitors to gently touch a prickly urchin or a starfish. An overview of whaling history includes a skeleton of a twenty-eight-foot gray whale yearling. Exhibits on the offshore drilling issue. Self-guided tours, brochure available.

Special programs include lectures, workshops, wet labs, field trips, classes, whale-watching trips, daily multimedia shows. The "Ocean Outreach" program by an accredited instructor offers a variety of classroom presentations for grades K–8.

A good brochure provides assistance in self-guided tours. School tours offered until 1 P.M. Auditorium, classroom, and laboratories. The gift shop offers books and gifts related to marine life. Gift shop open Tuesday–Sunday 11:30 A.M.–3 P.M. No restaurant. Park and beach nearby. Wheelchair access.

The marine museum is open year-round, Tuesday–Friday from noon–5 P.M., Saturday and Sunday 10 A.M.–5 P.M. Closed on Mondays and holidays. Admission is free. Parking fee of $4 at museum lot. Additional limited street parking. For more information call (213) 548-7562.

Catalina Island Museum

1 Casino Way, Avalon, Catalina Island, CA 90704

GETTING THERE: Visitors may reach Catalina Island by departing from San Pedro or Long Beach. From San Pedro go to the Port of Los Angeles under the Vincent Thomas Bridge. It can be reached by going south on the Harbor Fwy (I–110) to the Harbor Blvd. exit. From Long Beach the departure terminal is at Magnolia-Navy Landing, 330 Golden Shore Blvd. It can be reached by going south on the Long Beach Fwy (U.S. 7) almost to the end. Take the first downtown exit, then the Golden Shore exit. Parking is at both terminals. On the island, boat passengers disembark at Crescent Ave. Follow Crescent to the right, through town, to the large Casino Building. For boat reservations call (714) 527-7111 or for more information call the Catalina Chamber of Commerce at (213) 831-8822.

This museum is inside the famous Casino Building that was constructed in 1929 by William Wrigley, Jr., in Avalon, the only city on the island. A handsome landmark, it resembles a fortress overlooking the beautiful bay, and typical of many buildings in Avalon, its rooftop has tiles that were manufactured here from the early 1920s to 1943. A permanent exhibition inside the museum shows examples of tile designs from the island's former tile industry and types of pottery from that era. Most of the exhibits focus on natural history, archaeology, and settlement history of Santa Catalina Island, and include Indian and fishing artifacts. Also on view are ship models of the *Cabrillo* which transported visitors from Los Angeles Harbor between 1904 and 1941, the *Avalon* from 1920 to 1951, and the *Catalina* which was in service from 1924 until 1976. Other ship models are glass bottom fishing and touring boats. Rotating exhibitions are drawn from an extensive photography collection documenting the history of the island, and a topography map is of particular interest to visitors curious about the geography and natural environment of Catalina Island. The museum's library is open to the public and researchers may use the archives by appointment. In addition to films and lectures, the museum organizes tours of Holly Hill House, a Queen Anne-style residence built in 1890. Reservations are required for tours. Call (213) 510-2414.

No restaurants or picnic area. The bookstore offers a wide range of books about the Gabrieliño Indians and natural history of the Channel Islands. Wheelchair access.

Open daily. Wednesday and Saturday 10:30 A.M.–4 A.M., other days 1–4 P.M. From May to October Friday and Saturday hours include 7–9 P.M. Admission is free. For more information call (213) 510-2414.

Drum Barracks Civil War Museum
1052 Banning Blvd., Wilmington, CA 90744

GETTING THERE: From the Harbor Fwy (I-ll0) take the Pacific Coast Hwy exit and proceed one mile east to Avalon Blvd. Turn right on Avalon and continue to M St. Make a left onto M and continue to Banning Blvd.

The Drum Barracks are the last remaining evidence of the army established here in 1861 as a Civil War garrison and depot. A rendezvous for thousands of recruits for the Army of the West, it served the area which was to become southern California, Nevada, Arizona, and New Mexico. Named for Assistant Adjutant General Richard Coulter Drum, the camp was also used as a base for operations against the Indians. Models of the original camp are on display along with relic books of that period, a Gatlin gun, an 1855 sleigh bed, mahogany organ, and square grand piano. Free parking and admission. No eating facilities or gift shop. Special parking, ramps, and wheelchair access.

Museum hours are 1–3 P.M. on 2nd and 4th Saturdays of each month. Donations are welcome. For more information and to reserve tours, call (213) 548-7509 on weekdays, 9 A.M.–1 P.M.

Fort MacArthur Military Museum
Leavenworth Drive, San Pedro, CA 90731

GETTING THERE: The museum is located near the southern terminal of the Harbor Fwy (I–110). Take Gaffey St. to 36th St. and turn right onto Leavenworth Dr. into Angels Gate Park. Continue ¼ mile to the museum.

Coastal artillery and memorabilia from Civil War to World War II are displayed in this museum. Its location emphasizes the concern for coastal defense during World War II, and there is a permanent exhibition of a large civilian defense plan implemented at that time. Also on display are coast artillery and field artillery weapons and vehicles, 250 photographs, and miscellaneous memorabilia. A documentary film runs continually in the theater.

On the first Sunday of each month a group called "The Living History" parades in uniform and conducts coastal artillery exercises on the museum grounds. Annual events include the Fort MacArthur Artillery Show which displays and demonstrates field artillery weapons from the Revolutionary period through World War II. A lecture on local World War II history and Fort MacArthur is offered to school groups. The museum cosponsors a lecture tour with the City of Palos Verdes and Harbor College. In the near future the museum will develop a library and open a gift shop and bookstore. Picnic area. No wheelchair facilities.

The museum is open Saturday and Sunday and on national holidays, noon–5 P.M. Free admission and parking. Donations accepted. For more information or to reserve tours, call (213) 519-1874.

Lomita Railroad Museum
2135 West 250th St., Lomita, CA 90717

GETTING THERE: Take the Harbor Fwy (I–110) to the Lomita Blvd. or Pacific Coast Hwy exit. Go west. The museum is located between the Pacific Coast Hwy and Lomita Blvd. From Pacific Coast Hwy, go west to Narbonne Ave., north to 250th St., then east one block to Woodward Ave., and turn right.

Driving down residential Woodward Avenue in what seems to be an unlikely place for a railroad museum, museum-goers will suddenly see a full-scale Mogul locomotive directly ahead. Next to it is

Lomita Railroad Museum in residential Lomita. Photo by Sara LeBien.

the Lomita Railroad Museum, a charming replica of a small depot in Wakefield, Massachusetts. Outside are railroad cars, including a 1902 Mogul oil engine, 1910 caboose, a velocipede (a three-wheeled, one-man car used by track inspectors), a 1923 oil tank car and, across the street in a park annex, a 1913 boxcar.

On display inside the depot are collections of whistles, trainmen's uniform buttons, a collection of kerosene hand lanterns, and various color lights used to signal messages from train crew to engineer. There are link-and-pin couplers used by switchmen and brakemen, locomotive bells, and a locomotive builder's plate collection. Much like hallmarks on sterling silver pieces, these plates tell the name and location of the builder as well as the date of manufacture. This is just a small portion of the many collections and exhibitions in this beautiful little depot that railroading fans and children very much enjoy. The museum hosts an annual Camera Day. The gift shop sells jewelry, engineer caps, emblem patches, and railroad souvenirs. Street parking. Picnic area and wheelchair access.

No longer part of the museum, Little Engines, next door, is a delightful backyard track and shop for miniature train hobbyists specializing in parts for model steam-driven locomotives, plans, and castings.

Open Wednesday–Sunday 10 A.M.–5 P.M. Admission is 50¢. For more information or to reserve tours, call (213) 326–6255.

Long Beach Museum of Art
2300 East Ocean Blvd., Long Beach, CA 90803

GETTING THERE: Take the Long Beach Fwy (U.S. 7) to the Broadway exit (left), and follow to Cherry Ave. Turn right to Ocean Blvd. Turn left.

This museum is housed in a two-story craftsman-style mansion which sits on a bluff overlooking the ocean. Built in 1911, it was once a summer home. Concentrating on contemporary California artists, the permanent collection includes works by Masami Teraoka and Toyokuni, watercolors by Guy Williams, Feininger, and Kandinsky, and wood and marble works by Gwynn Murrell.

Contemporary California artists receive attention at the Long Beach Museum of Art. Photo by Sara LeBien.

A valuable collection of drawings by Poussin, Ingres, David Ligare, and Walkowitz, commonly known for his drawings of Isadora Duncan, and many works by Russian artist Alexej Jawlensky, graphics and minimalist sculpture, a German impressionist collection, and a selection of nineteenth- and twentieth-century works comprise the museum's permanent collection. Noteworthy video art exhibit. Tours available. Reservations required. The museum offers special programs to the public cosponsored by California State University. These include two video series, seminars, and workshops. The Artist's Market is held biannually. The video annex (5373 East 2nd Street) is a media arts center which houses a production studio and the largest West Coast collection of video art.

The museum gift shop in the carriage house has an assortment of jewelry, a children's section, and an enormous selection of art books. The gallery sells prints and posters as well as some apparel. No restaurant. Wheelchair access only on first floor. Free street parking.

Open Wednesday–Sunday noon–5 P.M. Closed Mondays, Tuesdays, and federal holidays. Donations appreciated. For more information call (213) 439-2119.

Los Angeles Maritime Museum
Berth 84, San Pedro, CA 90731

GETTING THERE: Take the Harbor Fwy (I–110) south to the end, beyond which it becomes Gaffey. Turn left on 5th St. The museum is at Harbor Blvd. and 5th St., near Ports of Call.

This very interesting museum, in a remodeled ferry building at the Los Angeles Harbor, exhibits a full range of maritime artifacts, models, and memorabilia. Two fascinating models, eighteen and fourteen feet long respectively, of the RMS *Titanic* and the RMS *Lusitania* with a cutaway view to reveal the ships' staterooms, dining salons, and engine rooms are accurately detailed. The *Lusitania* was used in filming *The Poseidon Adventure*.

The museum's major exhibitions feature navigational artifacts, diving helmets, ship models, illustrations, and paintings, as well as sailor's crafts produced over long whaling voyages, such as macrame, fancy knots, and scrimshaw. Special programs include film,

66

The "unsinkable" Los Angeles Maritime Museum. Photo by Sara LeBien.

This is just one of the many models on display at the Los Angeles Maritime Museum. Photo by Sara LeBien.

lectures, and workshops. Tours. Reservations required for schools
and large groups. The gift shop sells ship models, clocks, books,
model kits, posters, and scrimshaw reproductions.

Open Tuesday–Sunday 10 A.M.–5 P.M. Closed Mondays. Free admission and parking. For more information and for group tours, call (213) 548-7618.

Point Vicente Interpretive Center
31501 Palos Verdes Drive West, Rancho Palos Verdes, CA 90274

GETTING THERE: The museum is near the intersection of
Hawthorne Blvd. and Palos Verdes Drive West. Take the Harbor
Fwy (I-110) all the way south onto Gaffey. Turn west on 25th St.
and follow it all the way to Palos Verdes Drive West; or take scenic
Pacific Coast Hwy to the Palos Verdes Blvd. which turns into Palos
Verdes Drive West. The site is next to the Point Vicente
Lighthouse.

From this small museum perched on a bluff overlooking the ocean
at the tip of Rancho Palos Verdes, migrating whales can be
observed. The museum itself focuses on the geological and cultural
history of the Palos Verdes Peninsula and on the Pacific gray
whale. Historic displays show how the early Palos Verdes ranchos
served as trading posts and customs houses for passing ships. In
the Wonder of the Whale exhibition visitors can hear recordings of
the whale songs. Although the exhibition area is small, the displays are well done. A video monitor reveals up-to-date information about special events and visitor recreational services and
current data on whales sighted.

The whale-watch season runs from December through April, and
while some visitors are inside viewing displays, others are outside
with binoculars hoping to sight whale activity or strolling along the
quarter-mile path enjoying the spectacular coastline panorama. An
upper tower also offers good enclosed viewing.

The exhibits include fossils, a topographic map model, mounted
animals, artifacts, and photos pertaining to whales, geology, and
development of the harbor and peninsula. Lectures and classes are
available. "Whale of a Day" is held in January, and an annual event
is held each October. A school outreach program is being developed. Guided tours available. The gift shops sells photographs,

books on marine life, and art work. Ample picnic area on the bluff. Wheelchair access except in the tower. Free parking.

Open daily 10 A.M.–5 P.M. in winter and 10 A.M.–7 P.M. during the summer. Closed Thanksgiving, Christmas, and New Year's Day. Admission for adults $1, children 50¢. For more information and to reserve a group tour, call (213) 377-5370.

The *Queen Mary*
1126 Queen's Way, Pier J, Long Beach Harbor, CA 90802

GETTING THERE: Take the Long Beach Fwy (U.S. 7) south and follow the signs to the *Queen Mary*. You will see it from the freeway.

This is the world's largest oceanliner afloat and it is also a maritime museum. Exhibits, films, and models follow the pluralistic life of this great ship, from its days as a magnificent pleasure ship for the rich and famous to its use as a troop ship during World War II.

A good place to begin a visit on board is in the ship's theater on D Deck where a film and a multislide show document the *Queen Mary's* construction and launch. On display are original renderings of the ship plans in the 1920s and photographs taken during construction, final launch, the maiden voyage in 1936, and the tumultuous celebration upon its arrival in New York. Visitors will enjoy self-guided tours through the staterooms, barber shop, gymnasium, ballroom, wheelhouse, and engine room.

Another exhibit illustrates life aboard ship during World War II when 750,000 servicemen and women were transported nearly 600,000 miles. In the maritime heritage area an exhibit called "Ships of Destiny" is a historical display of the *Titanic, Lusitania, Andrea Doria, Normandy* and *Queen Elizabeth*. In contrast to these exhibits, the ship also houses a wonderful collection of art deco objects, etchings, art glass, alabaster, and bronze works of the 1920s. Still remaining from the ship's grand days are works of art, including paintings and bronzes, and wood carvings depicting the history of ship building.

Annual events include the *Queen Mary* Jazz Festival in May which has outgrown the ship and is now accommodated in the huge adjoining lot. Self-guided tours, also a guided tour for an additional $4, and an additional Captain's Tour of the art collection. Restaurant, coffee shop, and picnic area. Special parking and wheelchair access. Parking $3.

Open daily. Summer hours (June 22–Labor Day) are 9 A.M.–9 P.M.; box office closes at 8 P.M. General season hours are 10 A.M.–6 P.M.; box office closes at 4 P.M. Admission is $14.95 for adults, $8.50 for children 11 and under, $13.50 for senior citizens. Group rates are available to 20 or more on advance notice. Prices include admission to the *Spruce Goose* flying boat located at the same pier. For more information call (213) 435-3511.

Rancho Los Alamitos Historic Site and Gardens
6400 Bixby Hill Road, Long Beach, CA 90815

GETTING THERE: The San Diego Fwy (I-405), Garden Grove Fwy (22) and San Gabriel River Fwy (I-605) intersect about one mile southeast of the site. The ranch entrance is at the intersection of Anaheim Road and Palos Verdes Ave. in Long Beach. CSU-Long Beach is nearby.

Surrounded by lovely gardens and farm buildings, Long Beach's oldest adobe, with its original thick walls and handmade bricks, recalls the early days of farms and ranches in southern California. Built in 1806, it is one of the few remaining ranches in southern California that began its existence in the Spanish Colonial period serving under Spanish, Mexican, and American flags.

Fine furnishings, books, and art are displayed here as is an extensive collection of glass art. The adjoining barns and blacksmith shop are fully furnished with farm tools and equipment. Five acres of formal gardens surround the house. Wood-carved gates, clay pottery, old benches, wrought-iron works, and fountains throughout the garden exemplify Spanish and Mexican influence. Tours available. Reservations required for groups of ten or more. A research library is open to the public. The annual Creative Rancho Day presents typical activities on a ranch of the 1900s, with live demonstrations of blacksmithing, sheep shearing, and domestic skills. Citrus Day annually celebrates the citrus ranching period in Orange County with old citrus harvesting exhibits. School tours for third and fourth grade students may be scheduled on Wednesday, Thursday, and Friday mornings. No restaurant or gift shop on grounds, but two city parks nearby provide picnic areas.

Open Wednesday–Sunday 1–5 P.M. Closed Mondays and Tuesdays. Free parking and admission. For more information call (213) 431–3541.

Rancho Los Cerritos Museum
4600 Virginia Road, Long Beach, CA 90807

GETTING THERE: Accessible from Long Beach Fwy (U.S. 7) or San Diego Fwy (I–405). From I–405, exit at Long Beach Blvd. Go north to San Antonio Dr. Turn left, then right onto Virginia Road.

This handsome, two-story Spanish Colonial adobe preserves an atmosphere of the 1870s when it was a major sheep and cattle ranch of 28,000 acres. Inside the house are typical Victorian furnishings and period costumes and a library specializing in California history. At the visitors center one may find rotating exhibits of costumes, toys, photographs, quilts, historical documentation, and carpenter and blacksmith's tools. Tours available. Reservations required for groups of ten or more.

Lectures and workshops for the public. Annual events include 1870s Ranch Christmas by Candlelight, and an Easter Egg Hunt. Fourth-grade school program and hands-on presentation. Gift shop and picnic areas on grounds. Wheelchair access in most areas, special parking, and restrooms.

Open Wednesday–Sunday 1–5 P.M. Closed Mondays and Tuesdays. Free admission and parking. For more information call (213) 424–9423.

Spruce Goose Flying Boat
1126 Queen's Way, Pier J, Long Beach Harbor, Long Beach, CA 90802

GETTING THERE: Take Long Beach Fwy (U.S. 7) south to the Port of Long Beach. Located next to the *Queen Mary*.

This is an aeronautical museum actually installed inside the world's largest airplane. Designed and built by Howard Hughes to carry cargo and troops during World War II, it has a wing span of 320 feet and a tail reaching eight stories high. It carried enough fuel for an average car to drive around the world fifteen times! Exhibits comprise Howard Hughes' flying boat, aircraft replicas, and memorabilia. Besides the flying boat there are full scale replicas of the

H-1 Racer, the Wright Brothers' model B-Flyer, and an operating cutaway Pratt and Whitney R4360 engine. In addition are Hughes' aviation trophies and personal memorabilia. A multimedia presentation highlights his life as well as the history of the *Spruce Goose*. A new multivisual show, "Ships of Flight," looks at the natural history of flight and provides an overview of aviation history, from early pioneers of the science to space technology. Restaurant, coffee shop, and picnic area. Special parking and wheelchair access. Parking is $3 for autos, $5 for oversized vehicles.

Open daily year-round 10 A.M.–6 P.M. The box office is open until 5 P.M. Admission to the *Spruce Goose* and *Queen Mary* is $14.50 for adults, $8.50 for children 11 and under, $13.05 for senior citizens. For more information call (213) 435-3511.

University Art Museum, Long Beach
1250 Bellflower Blvd., Long Beach, CA 90840

GETTING THERE: From the San Diego Fwy (I-405), the San Gabriel River Fwy (I-605), or the Garden Grove Fwy (22), exit onto 7th St. west. Turn right at the fourth stoplight (West Campus Road) and right again at the first street. Proceed to the visitor information booth at the north end of the parking circle. The museum is located on the fifth floor of the campus library. The Bellflower Blvd. mailing address is *not* the location of the museum.

In 1986 the California Arts Council ranked this museum among the top six arts institutions in the state, calling it a "model for university museums." A monumental sculpture collection is on view throughout the 320-acre campus, including works by Robert Irwin, Clare Falkenstein, Bryan Hunt, Gabriel Kohn, Piotr Kowalski, Guy Dill, Robert Murphy, Tom Van Sant, Richard Turner, Kengiro Axuma, J. J. Beljon, Andre Bloc, and Woods Davy. Temporary installations of other sculpture may also be seen throughout the campus. A brochure guides visitors to the sculpture, covering about two miles of landscaped pathways.

Known for its diverse, creative exhibitions, the museum invites artists to experiment and introduce innovative works never seen before on the West Coast, and through this program significant works have emerged. Some of the artists who have been featured here include Laurie Anderson, Francesco Clemente, Laddie John

Dill, Barbara Kasten, Robert Motherwell, Susan Rothenberg, Wayne Thiebaud, and William Wedman.

The museum's permanent collection includes works on paper by Leland Rice, Frances Benjamin Johnston, David Hockney, Laddie John Dill, George Segal, Jim Dine, Joe Deal, Judy Fiskin, Kenneth McGowan, Grant Medford, Roy Lichtenstein, Frank Stella, and Tony Hernandez.

In addition to its major exhibition, every six weeks the museum offers a broad range of opportunities to explore the art world in southern California by visiting studios, galleries, museums, and historical sites. "Noon in the Gallery" is a series of informal lectures held on the Wednesday following the opening of each exhibition, and videotapes of some lectures can be viewed by appointment. Hands-on children's programs are also presented. Reservations are required for guided tours. Call (213) 498-5761. Educational programs are "Art to the Schools," "Art to the People," "Discover Long Beach," "Art Partners," and scheduled tours. The bookstore and museum shop offer a selection of handmade jewelry, catalogs, and art-related books. There is no restaurant in the building. Wheelchair access. Parking is by permit only during the week. Weekend parking is free. For special event parking, call the museum.

Open Tuesday–Saturday 11 A.M.–5 P.M., Sunday 1–5 P.M. Closed Mondays. Donation of $1 for adults, 50¢ for seniors and children. For more information call (213) 498-5761.

Chapter Four

Coastal Orange County

Laguna Art Museum
307 Cliff Dr., Laguna Beach, CA 92651

GETTING THERE: From the San Diego Fwy south (I-405) take Route 133 and go west to the Pacific Coast Hwy, then north. The museum is located on the corner of Pacific Coast and Cliff Dr., in the heart of Laguna Beach.

In 1918, a free-spirited group of artists living in tents at Laguna Beach indirectly began this museum. After outgrowing their first exhibition gallery in the Old Town Hall, they moved into the present site. The building and its name changed a few times during the years as it gained prominence, and the latest expansion has added nine new galleries and a greenhouse entrance which adds distinction to the pink-stuccoed corner building.

Known for its focus on emerging southern California artists, who from 1918 to 1928 painted a historical account of California that brought them East Coast recognition, the museum's real emphasis is on representing all periods and schools of California art. In addition is a contemporary photography collection which grew from the acquisition of early works by Paul Outerbridge.

The sculpture collection is also expanding with the addition of one hundred works. Southern California artists commissioned to design both outdoor and indoor sculptures, are combining a variety of materials such as marble, terrazzo, glass, concrete, copper, and aluminum. One such abstract piece, designed by Michael Davis, is compatible with the interior design of the building, but also extends through the exterior front wall and is integrated with the outside design as well. Tours by reservation. Street parking. Several restaurants nearby. Wheelchair access.

Open Tuesday–Sunday 11 A.M.–5 P.M. Closed Mondays. Admission is $2 for adults, $1 for senior citizens, children under 12 free. For more information call (714) 494–8971 or (714) 494–6531. The museum also has an annex in South Coast Plaza, a shopping center just off I–405 at the Brixtol exit. Their hours are Monday–Friday 11 A.M.–6 P.M., and noon–5 P.M. on weekends. For a recorded message call (714) 494–6531 or for more information call (714) 494–8971.

Mission San Juan Capistrano Museum

31882 Camino Capistrano, San Juan Capistrano, CA 92675

GETTING THERE: From the San Diego Fwy (I–405) continue south to the Ortega Hwy (74) exit, turn west and continue 2½ blocks. The museum is located at the corner of Ortega Hwy and Camino Capistrano.

Founded in 1980, this is a hands-on historical museum that provides educational opportunities for learning about southern California heritage. The museum's living history programs study the early Juaneño Indians, the Spanish influence in California, and the Rancho Period. As part of this, archaeologists, students, and volunteers participate in the discovery of Native American and colonial artifacts at the archaeological sites on the premises. Visitors may tour this area to view these findings. Also an educational garden of precolonial plants and cactus.

This eight-room museum, housed in the west wing of the mission, displays wall-size historic murals, including one that depicts the 1769 Portola Expedition entering Capistrano Valley, making the first contact between Europeans and local Native Americans. It also contains Native American and Hispanic objects.

A soldiers' barracks is being restored and a Rancho-period room is also underway, as are areas on the museum grounds that will re-create the daily work of Native Americans and Spaniards over 200 years ago. Lectures and workshops. Gift shop sells religious items. Picnic area in nearby Caspers Park and Doheny State Beach. Wheelchair access. Street parking.

Open daily 8 A.M.–4:30 P.M. Admission is $2 for adults, 50¢ for children. For more information call (714) 496–4720.

Extracting a fossil at Natural History Museum of Orange County. Courtesy of museum.

Natural History Museum of Orange County
2627 Vista Del Oro, Newport Beach, CA 92660

GETTING THERE: From the San Diego Fwy (I–405) take MacArthur Blvd. exit. Go south to Jamboree Road, then west to Eastbluff Dr. Turn right and continue to the second stop sign at Vista Del Oro and turn right.

One of the prominent exhibits at this museum is the Insect Zoo, a constantly changing exhibit on the life cycle of many fascinating species. Other displays feature fossils, colorful minerals, a small dinosaur casting of Tyrannosaurus rex, early pottery from the Gabrieliño Indians, and historic artifacts, including specimens taken from a nearby Miocene fossil bed. Films and lectures. Fossil laboratory open Tuesday and Saturday 10 A.M.–3 P.M. and Thursday 10 A.M.–3 P.M. and 6–9 P.M. Tours available. Reservations required. Adult classes cosponsored with local colleges. Gift shop. Picnic area. Wheelchair access and parking.

Open Tuesday–Saturday 10 A.M.–5 P.M. Closed Sundays and Mondays. Free admission and parking. For more information call (714) 640-7120.

Nautical Heritage Museum
24532 Del Prado Blvd., Dana Point, CA 92629

GETTING THERE: From the north, take the San Diego Fwy (I–405) south to the Pacific Coast Hwy (north) and Camino Los Ramblas exit. Follow Pacific Coast Hwy west to Amber St. Turn left and go to Del Prado. Turn left on Del Prado which is the southbound Pacific Coast Hwy through Dana Point.

The New England lighthouse design of this building recently received a beautification award. Inside, the Nautical Heritage Society houses permanent exhibits of original documents of famous seafarers, more than one hundred historical ship models, weapons, and other nautical artifacts and photographs. One interesting display explains the history of scrimshaw.

Adhering to its original goal of perpetuating "an awareness and interest in nautical heritage of the West Coast of the United States," the society's main focus is on an unusual educational program through which teachers and high school and college students receive nautical training and appreciation of the coastal environment. This is accomplished through sailing programs on thirty ships including the *Californian*, the state's official tallship (old-style sailing ship with square sails). At various dockside ports up and down the coast and at Dana Point, visitors may view this ship.

Brief museum tours are available. Unusual works of art with a nautical theme are available in the gift shop. No restaurant. Free street parking and parking lot in rear. No wheelchair access.

Open Tuesday–Saturday 10 A.M.–4 P.M. Closed Sundays and Mondays. Free admission. For more information call (714) 661-1001.

Newport Harbor Museum
850 San Clemente Dr., Newport Beach, CA 92660

GETTING THERE: From the San Diego Fwy (I–405) take MacArthur Blvd. (Rte 73) south to San Joaquin Hills Road. Turn right and go to Jamboree Road. Turn left and left again at Santa Barbara Dr. and left on San Clemente.

With the expectation of educating their viewers on the roots of contemporary art, the Newport Museum offers a broad exhibition program on the history of modern art. Showing modern trends which reveal these foundations, the exhibitions and special programs make this much more than a gallery of fine arts. The permanent collection, shown in six major shows per year, focuses on American and California artists since 1945. Three shows also showcase new California artists. Films, workshops, and lectures. Docent outreach program and contemporary culture series. Restaurant. Free parking. Small art pieces for sale in shop. Wheelchair access and parking.

Open daily 10 A.M.–5 P.M. Admission is $3 for adults, $2 for children and senior citizens, under 6 free. For more information call (714) 759-1122.

Chapter Five

Inland Orange County

Anaheim Museum

241 South Anaheim Blvd., Anaheim, CA 92805

GETTING THERE: Exit the Santa Ana Fwy (I–5) at Lincoln Ave. Go east to Anaheim Blvd, turn left. The museum is on the right.

Located in the newly renovated 1908 Carnegie Library Building, the Anaheim Museum is the last of five such buildings in Orange County financed by philanthropist Andrew Carnegie. A museum of general history, the emphasis is on local history and displays Anaheim artifacts, costumes, and fossils. Rotating exhibitions in the permanent Anaheim Room focus on aspects of Anaheim's history, including its citrus production and the development of Disneyland, professional sports, and local industries. A children's gallery presents hands-on exhibits every three months, with projects such as the working of a loom or printing press. The museum also hosts major traveling exhibitions from the Smithsonian Institute. The current collection of 5,000 objects includes many artifacts related to the city's ethnic history, particularly when it was a German community.

Docents bearing trunkfuls of museum paraphernalia and displays will visit local elementary schools by arrangement, and exhibits can be loaned to other institutions. Films, lectures, and workshops. Tours available by reservation. Book and gift shop. No restaurant or picnic area. Wheelchair access and elevator. Street parking and parking structure across the street.

Open Wednesday–Sunday 10 A.M.–4 P.M. Closed Mondays, Tuesdays, and all holidays. Admission is $1.50 for adults, $1 for senior citizens, children under 12 with an adult free. Military with ID free. For more information call (714) 778-3301.

Bowers Museum
2002 North Main St., Santa Ana, CA 92706

GETTING THERE: From the Santa Ana Fwy (I–5), take the 17th St. exit and continue west ½ mile to Main St., then turn right. The museum is located at the corner of 20th and Main streets.

Charles Bowers was a prosperous citrus grower and land developer during the late nineteenth century. Out of gratitude for the land that had brought him good fortune, Bowers and his wife Ada established a trust for a museum to be built that would feature 200 years of Orange County's history. The museum opened in 1936 and has expanded the scope and quantity of its collection to a present total of over two million objects. Since 1974 the museum has also acquired many African, Oceanic, and pre-Columbian works of art. Western Americana is also represented in the museum's collection of paintings, sculptures, and artifacts. The museum installs multicultural displays of art and artifacts from Native North and South America, Africa, the Pacific Basin, and Oceania.

Annual events include outstanding art shows, and visiting exhibitions from the Smithsonian Institute and the American Federation of the Arts. Films, lectures, workshops, hands-on workshops for all ages, and travel opportunities available. Group tours from October through June by appointment.

Beginning in December 1988, a $12 million expansion program of 33,000 square feet will include new galleries, a restaurant, and an auditorium. The museum exhibitions will temporarily be on view at two satellite locations. Call for information.

Open Tuesday–Saturday 10 A.M.–5 P.M., Sunday noon–5 P.M. For more information call (714) 972-1900 or (714) 547-8304 for a recorded message.

Children's Museum at La Habra
301 South Euclid, La Habra, CA 92632

GETTING THERE: From the Pomona Fwy (60), take the Orange Fwy (57) south to Lambert exit. Turn right, continue west to Euclid and turn right. From the Santa Ana Fwy (I–5), exit at Euclid and head north to the museum.

Bowers Museum. Photo by Sara LeBien.

Mural on exterior wall of Bowers Museum highlights Orange County history. Photo by Sara LeBien.

This museum for children is mainly a hands-on and participatory learning center. Equipped with piano, dollhouse, books, and games, the center encourages play activities that coincide with educational exhibits. Formerly a Union Pacific Railroad depot, the museum has several railroad cars on display outside. There is also a wildlife exhibit, a baggage room displaying a model train and village, and historical artifacts in the caboose. Other permanent exhibits include Grandma's Attic, Playspace, Festival of Japan, and Under the Big Top. Lectures, workshops, and tours by reservation. Annual auction and children's art festival. Nature walk, bee observatory, and Saturday afternoon programs for children. Groups of ten or more by reservation only. Gift shop. Picnic area. Wheelchair access.

Open Tuesday–Saturday 10 A.M.–4 P.M. Admission is $1.50 for adults, $1 for children under 16, and senior citizens. For more information call (213) 946–9793.

The Fullerton Museum Center
301 North Pomona Ave., Fullerton, CA 92632

GETTING THERE: Take the Artesia Fwy (91) to the Harbor Blvd. exit. Go north to Wilshire Blvd. and turn right to Pomona Ave. The museum is on the corner of Pomona and Wilshire, one block east of Harbor Blvd.

A grand reopening in March 1988 climaxed a major renovation of this thirty-year-old former library. The Spanish Colonial Revival structure is a designated historical landmark and has three galleries totaling nearly 4,200 square feet. A lecture room with a small stage seats seventy-five and is the location for cultural and educational events.

Retaining its emphasis on science, technology, history, and cultural arts, the museum houses traveling exhibitions as well as changing exhibits and permanent exhibitions of an extensive eighteenth- and nineteenth-century costume and textile collection representing both American and European fashion. Many once belonged to the founding families of Orange County and are creations of world-famous fashion designers.

A broad scope of art is represented, from needle art to laser photography, and includes Shaker craftsmanship, video art, and

This 1890 J. Frederick Worth gown is part of an extensive costume collection at the Fullerton Museum Center. Courtesy of museum.

miniatures. Demonstrations of these works are presented during the run of the exhibitions. Educational programs offer lectures, workshops, and tours. Reservations are necessary for guided tours. The museum gift shop sells stationery, prints, unusual gifts. Wheelchair access, free parking, and picnic area.

Open Tuesday and Wednesday 11 A.M.–4 P.M., Thursday and Friday 1–9 P.M., Saturday and Sunday 11 A.M.–4 P.M. Closed Mondays and major holidays. Admission is $2 for adults and students, children under 12 free. For more information call (714) 738-6545.

Heritage Hill Historical Park
25151 Serrano Road, El Toro, CA 92705

GETTING THERE: From the Santa Ana (I–5) or San Diego (I–405) freeways take Lake Forest Dr. exit east to Serrano. Turn left.

Four historic structures in this three-acre park trace local history from the era of Mexican ranchos to the beginning of the citrus industry in Orange County, when the early English settlers came here to become gentlemen fruit farmers. The only Spanish influence can be seen in the adobe, the one structure that was original to the property. Handmade clay bricks remain on its floor. The Bennett Ranch house has much of the original furnishings of the Bennett family, and their grandchildren have been instrumental in acquiring additional pieces for the house.

Built in 1891, the Episcopal Mission was used for worship by the English settlers, and some of its original furnishings include the oak baptismal font with clamshell basin, a carved altar, and a reed organ. A one-room schoolhouse, the first in the El Toro area, is furnished authentically and is the site for a living history program for fourth graders, who may spend an abbreviated typical day in a rancho-era school. The docent acting as school marm will explain early customs and uses of antique items. Tour available. A visitors center has been added to house permanent and changing exhibitions pertaining to El Toro history, and a citrus grove, representing the flourishing citrus industry, has been replanted. No restaurant. Wheelchair access on outdoor tours.

Open daily 8 A.M.–5 P.M. Free admission and parking. For more information call (714) 855-2028.

Historic George Key Ranch

625 West Bastanchury Road, Placentia, CA 92670

GETTING THERE: Take the Orange Fwy (57) north to the Yorba Linda Blvd. exit. Turn right (east) and follow to Placentia Ave. Turn left and left again on Bastanchury Road. Continue beyond the ranch to Gilman Circle to park.

The house and barn furnishings are typical of citrus ranch and farm life of the 1800s. To preserve the history of the citrus industry in Orange County, this citrus grower's home and two of the original twelve acres of orange groves are now open to the public. The two-story house dates from 1898 and was built by George B. Key, a Canadian who came here to superintend a citrus company in the Placentia area.

Three separate buildings house the kitchen and bedroom collections. On view in the bedrooms are furnishings typical of the late 1800s, including quilts and coal and oil lamps. A blacksmith shop represents the single-board wood structures typical in this era and area, where lumber was scarce. Artifacts from the early house and neighbor ranches are displayed.

An extensive collection of farm implements includes equipment used for plowing, planting, cultivating, harvesting, and citrus farming. Key's carpentry shop houses his extensive collection of tools for carpentry, smithing, and packaging citrus crops. The Verse Garden, begun by George G. Key, includes a collection of specimen trees and ground cover of flowers, shrubs, and sword ferns. Excerpts from Mr. Key's verse appear along garden walks.

Food and beverages are prohibited on the property, and there are no restroom facilities or drinking fountains. There is no shop, no restaurant, and no wheelchair access. Free parking. Because the house is occupied, entrance is by appointment and guided tour only on the second Wednesday of each month. Arrangements must be made at least three weeks in advance. Limited to twenty people per group. Call (714) 634-7420.

Admission is free. For more information call (714) 528-4260.

Modern Museum of Art
Griffin Towers, 5 Hutton Centre Dr., Santa Ana, CA 92707

GETTING THERE: From Newport Fwy (55), take the MacArthur exit and go west to Hutton Centre Dr. Turn left and go to Griffin Towers. The museum is on the ground floor.

This brand new fine arts museum exhibits art normally unavailable in this area. Contemporary Chinese realism, and works by Diego Rivera and Rufino Tomayo are some of its offerings. While developing its permanent collections, the museum's major focus is on educational outreach programs, using modern communications technology. This is the "modern" part of the museum's name; its acquisitions are not limited to modern art. A sculpture garden will also be developed. The gift shop offers books, catalogs, gift items, and unique pieces of jewelry and ceramics. Guided tours, with reservations, lectures, and films. Picnic area in sculpture garden. Free parking.

Open weekdays 10 A.M.–6 P.M., Saturday and Sunday noon–5 P.M. Free admission. For more information call (714) 754-4111.

Mott Miniatures
Knott's Berry Farm, 8039 Beach Blvd., Buena Park, CA 90620

GETTING THERE: From the Artesia/Riverside Fwy (91), exit south on Beach Blvd. Go one block to La Palma. The museum is located at Beach and La Palma.

The history of domestic life in America is presented here in miniature. Seventy years ago an eight-year-old girl named Allegra Mitchell opened a box of Cracker Jacks and was so charmed by the prize inside that she saved it—and hundreds more like it. This hobby grew into a lifetime interest in miniatures that she shared with her husband, Dewitt Mott, and their daughters. During the Depression, Dewitt Mott began to reproduce in miniature their own furniture, and as the collection grew he built miniature cabinets for the small treasures. The project is now called "History of the American Home" and comprises six houses that display how daily domestic life has been changed from the colonial period to the present. The series includes a pilgrim cabin, a 1750 eastern cabin, a Civil War-period house, a 1900 Golden Oak-period home, and a twentieth-century home.

There is also a display of miniature, fully operating power tools, fishing pole, reels, and even miniature flies. The "Beyond Belief" forest display of fairies and flowers is a light-hearted departure from the historic replicas. Lectures and guided tours. Annual events include a Halloween Haunt and a country fair. Restaurant and gift shop. Wheelchair access. Free parking nearby.

Open daily year-round. Winter hours: 10 A.M.–6 P.M. on weekdays, , 10 A.M.–11 P.M. on Saturday, 10 A.M.–7 P.M. on Sunday. Summer hours: 10 A.M.–11 P.M. on weekdays, 10 A.M.–1 A.M. on Saturday, 10 A.M.–9 P.M. on Sunday. For admittance only to the Mott Miniatures, go to Knott's Berry Farm's Guest Relations. Pay a refundable deposit of $17, and obtain a shopper's pass good for 30 minutes in Motts Miniatures. For more information call (714) 827-1776 or (714) 527-1843.

Movieland Wax Museum
7711 Beach Blvd., Buena Park, CA 90620

GETTING THERE: Exit the Santa Ana Fwy (I-5) or the Artesia/ Riverside Fwy (91) at the Beach Blvd. exit, going south. Museum is located between La Palma and Orangethorpe avenues, one block north of Knott's Berry Farm.

This entertaining museum is a collection of 130 realistic movie scenes with 231 lifelike wax figures of famous stars. On view is the set for *Dr. Zhivago,* with its reproduced snowbanks; the capsized ship in *The Poseidon Adventure,* and the bridge and crew of the Starship Enterprise. TV stars and comedians are also portrayed. In the "Chamber of Horrors" scenes from *The Exorcist, Psycho, The Phantom of the Opera,* as well as Dracula and Frankenstein, can send chills up your spine. The good old days are represented by Rudolph Valentino and *The Wizard of Oz.* This tour through the maze of walkways immortalizes seventy years of the movie industry.

Annual events include special set dedications, when stars visit the museum. Three gift shops sell Hollywood-related souvenirs and limited edition plates and figurines. Free parking. Pizza restaurant. Wheelchair access.

Open daily in summer 9 A.M.–10 P.M., winter 10 A.M.–9 P.M. Admission is $8.95 for adults, seniors $6.50, children $5.95 and under 4 free. Call (714) 522-1155 or (714) 522-1154 for a recorded message.

Will the real George Burns please sit down? Courtesy Movieland Wax Museum.

Whitaker-Jaynes and Bacon Houses
(Buena Park Historical Society)
7842 Whitaker St., Buena Park, CA 90621

GETTING THERE: Take Santa Ana Fwy (I-5) to the Beach Blvd. exit. Go east to Stanton and north to Whitaker.

Two historic houses occupy this site, now a small park. The main structure, the Whitaker-Jaynes House, is a two-story house, built around 1887, and was lived in by the brother of Buena Park's founder, prior to the Jaynes family. Behind the main house is the tiny Bacon House, the oldest house in Buena Park. Resembling a large playhouse, it consists of two rooms with the original furniture still intact.

In the main house are period furnishings and decorative arts, with rotating exhibits of an extensive collection of toys, dolls, china, silver, and crystal. Among the furnishings are an 1892 highchair, a beautiful square rosewood piano, and a milliner's cabinet. On permanent display is a collection of First Lady dolls dressed in accurate reproductions of their Inaugural ball gowns. A popular rotating exhibit, "What Is It?", displays such novelties as an 1893 snowcone maker.

Educational services include a "Carpet Bag Museum" outreach presentation of Victorian period artifacts. An Old Tyme Picnic (pot luck) is held the third Sunday in May. Reservations required for group tours. Picnic area. Wheelchair access to ground floor of main house. Free parking.

Open Thursday 10:30 A.M.-2:30 P.M. and the second Sunday of each month 1-4 P.M. Closed holidays. Donations appreciated. For more information, call (714) 521-9900, ext. 302.

The Whitaker-Jaynes House at Buena Park Historical Society Museum takes you back to the late 1800s. Photo by Sara LeBien.

Chapter Six

La Jolla and San Diego Areas

Antique Gas and Steam Engine Museum, Inc.

2040 North Santa Fe, Vista, CA 92083

GETTING THERE: From the north, take Escondido Fwy (I-15) south to Route 76. Follow it all the way to Santa Fe Ave. (S14). Turn left and continue to museum. From the south, take Escondido Fwy to Anza Fwy (Rte 78). Exit at Escondido Ave./ Sunset Dr. Turn right, and then left on Santa Fe. Go through town past Bobier Dr. to the museum.

Located on forty acres of rolling land in South Guajome County Park, this museum preserves early American farm life. Established in 1975 by the California Early Day Gas Engine and Tractor Association, the museum houses a collection of over 1,000 pieces of historical gas, steam, and horse-powered equipment relating to agriculture, lumbering, mining, oil drilling, and construction. In addition is a farmhouse with a country kitchen and parlor, and a complete blacksmith shop. Two annual events, the Threshing Bee and the Antique Engine Show, demonstrate early farm activities of planting, harvesting, threshing, log sawing, quilting, and butter churning. Also featured are folk dancing, American crafts, and traditional music. Square dancing and clogging can be viewed, and a vintage clothing fashion show is presented. An antique tractor parade occurs daily, and ⅓ scale train rides are available. Tours. Picnic area. Gift shop. Wheelchair access.

Open daily 10 A.M.–4 P.M. Free admission and parking. For more information and to reserve tours, call (619) 941-1791.

Cabrillo National Monument

Catalina Blvd., Point Loma, San Diego, CA 92106

GETTING THERE: Take Mission Valley Fwy/Ocean Beach Fwy (I-8) or San Diego Fwy (I-5) to Rosecrans St. exit. Go south and follow to Canon. Turn right and go to Catalina Blvd. Turn left and follow to monument entrance.

Four points of interest on this site include a statue commemorating the 1542 discovery of the California coast and San Diego Bay by Juan Rodriguez Cabrillo, a nineteenth-century lighthouse, a visitors center, and the museum. The visitors center portrays the life story of Captain Israel, the lighthouse keeper, and his wife. The museum exhibits pertain to the bravery and determination of early Spanish explorers. A large wall map charts Spanish expeditions throughout North America. The museum displays interesting nautical instruments probably used during the Spanish voyage, and a fine model of the *San Salvador,* Cabrillo's ship. A short walk up the hill leads visitors to the Point Loma Lighthouse with its rooms of attractive nineteenth-century furnishings. Surprisingly spacious and cozy, the living room, kitchen, and pantry are located on the ground level, with two bedrooms up the winding stairwell, and the tower with its prism light accessible by an extended ladder.

From this hilltop site is a spectacular view of San Diego Bay and its extensive naval and pleasure boat activity. Visitors may see helicopter exercises and precision flying from this vantage point. Whale sightings during the migration period are at least as fascinating as the museum exhibits. The gift shop offers a large selection of books on whales, marine life, plant life, and California history as well as prints and other gifts. The museum shows films on whales and Cabrillo history. Education programs available. Wheelchair access.

Open daily 9 A.M.–5 P.M. Free admission and parking. For more information call (619) 557-5450.

Lighthouse, Cabrillo National Monument, Point Loma. Photo by Sara LeBien.

Children's Museum of San Diego
8657 Villa La Jolla Dr., La Jolla, CA 92037

GETTING THERE: From the San Diego Fwy (I–5), take the La Jolla Village Dr. exit. Turn west and continue ½ mile to Villa La Jolla Dr. Go south to La Jolla Village Square, a shopping center. The museum is located on the lower level of the enclosed mall near the May Company.

"To see, to touch, to experience" is the purpose of this learning center museum, geared to ages four through twelve years old. Located in a large shopping center, this participatory museum has exhibits that are designed as hands-on areas rather than passive visual displays. Children may operate an old-fashioned switchboard, pilot an airplane, discover geometric shapes, or build cities with a seemingly endless supply of Legos. Art expression can be observed in the art studio and the internal organs of a torso can be explored in the Health Center. Role-playing is done in the doctor's office, the dentist's chair, or with the help of a wide selection of costumes. A popular exhibit is the television studio where children can read the weather report while being seen on a real television monitor. Gift shop sells a wide selection of educational and creative toys and materials. Restaurants in shopping mall. Wheelchair access. Mall parking.

Open Wednesday–Friday and Sunday noon–5 P.M., and 10 A.M.–5 P.M. on Saturday. Open Tuesday for group visits only. Closed Mondays and holidays. Admission is $2.50 for adults, $1 for senior citizens, children under 12 free. For more information call (619) 450–0767.

Imperial Valley College Museum
442 Main St., Imperial, CA 92251

GETTING THERE: Imperial is located midway between San Diego and Yuma, Arizona. Take Mission Valley Fwy (I–8) east to U.S. 86. Go north through El Centro to Main St. of Imperial, then west ½ block.

In an expanse of desert between San Diego and Arizona, major paleontology research is underway, and the permanent exhibitions at the museum represent this study with fossils found in the area. One rare find, the skeleton of a full-sized, one-million-year-old horse, is on display as are whale skeletons which were found in desert fossil beds.

Other exhibits pertain to anthropology, archaeology, and ethnographic findings. A showing of prehistoric tools represents the archaeological focus in major exhibitions that change every two years. Lectures. Tours. Reservations required for groups. Annual events include semiannual field trip, book sale, and semiannual pottery sale. Education services include outreach presentation to schools, community service clubs, etc. Gift shop. No restaurant. Wheelchair access. Street parking.

Open weekdays 8 A.M.–5 P.M. Saturdays by appointment only. Free admission. For more information call (619) 352-1667.

Imperial Valley Pioneers Museum
Imperial County Fairgrounds, Imperial, CA 92251

GETTING THERE: Take Mission Valley Fwy (I–8) east to U.S. 86. Go north through El Centro to Imperial.

This museum has a little bit of everything. It is located on the Fairgrounds in the small town of Imperial and is the only local history museum within a large vicinity, serving also as a local history archive. It focuses mainly on the agricultural valley which was reclaimed from the desert. Visitors can see a section of the old plank road that was constructed across Sand Hills, probably the only one of its kind ever built. Part of the first transcontinental road across the United States, it was used from 1914 to 1926. Another portion of it is on display at the Smithsonian.

An assortment of local history artifacts, photographs, Cocopah and Yuma Indian artifacts, desert paintings, pioneer tools, household furnishings and outside exhibits devoted to specialized farm equipment will prove interesting to western history buffs. After viewing the museum exhibitions, visitors may want to use the museum's self-guided tour map to visit some of the thirty-nine historic sites located in Imperial County. This brochure map is available at Chambers of Commerce in El Centro, Holtville, and Brawley. Outreach program to schools include slide presentations. Archives open by appointment four days a week for researchers. Call

(619) 352–3139 or 352–3078. Tour reservations required. Call (619) 356–1604. Fairgrounds picnic area. Wheelchair access.

The museum is open from October to May on Tuesday, Thursday, and Saturday 8 A.M.–noon, and 1–5 P.M. on Sunday. Free admission and parking. For more information call (619) 355–1222.

Julian Pioneer Museum
2811 Washington St., Julian, CA 92036

GETTING THERE: Julian is northeast of San Diego and sixty miles south of Los Angeles. From Los Angeles take the Escondido Fwy (I–15) to the Poway Road exit. Go left and follow twenty–two miles to the town of Ramona. Poway Road becomes Julian Road. Continue another twenty–two miles to Julian. The road becomes Washington St.

The community of Julian was developed in 1880 following the discovery of gold by Mike Julian. Reflecting that exciting history, the museum displays a little bit of everything which once belonged to its pioneer families and to neighboring San Diego Indians. Known as "Julian's little attic," the museum is in the former historic brewery built of rock. It houses turn-of-the-century clothing, household furnishings, machine and woodworking tools, and mining equipment. Also on view are spinning wheels used by the pioneer women, and some of their hand-loomed weavings. The lacework collection shows a variety of elaborate tatting and bobbin lace. Indian artifacts on display include buckskin clothing, beaded belts, and moccasins. Porcelain French and German dolls and an exhibition of mounted animals representative of the outlying rural area are also displayed.

The gift shop has a wide assortment of books on the California deserts and wildflowers. There is no restaurant, but the county park adjacent is available for picnics. Wheelchair access. Street parking.

Open daily during the summer, 10 A.M.–4 P.M. and during the winter on weekends and holidays except for Thanksgiving, Christmas, and New Year's Day. Closed if there is snow. Contributions are welcomed. For more information call (619) 765–0227.

La Jolla Museum of Contemporary Art
700 Prospect St., La Jolla, CA 92037

GETTING THERE: From the San Diego Fwy (I-5) take the Ardath exit north, or at La Jolla Village Dr. go south. From Ardath, turn right on Hidden Valley Road, left on Pines Road and right on Prospect. The museum is located at the intersection of Silverado and Draper streets.

The architecture of this beautiful museum lends itself to the contemporary works it displays. Situated on a bluff, the back of the building overlooks the sculpture garden immediately below, and the ocean beyond. A series of stark white galleries with glistening white floors present the large canvases of contemporary works, and includes photography, sculpture, and textile art. The primary collections consist of post-1950 minimalist, pop, post-minimalist, and abstract expressionist styles.

The museum presents a broad program of exhibitions and video art, and is known for its in-depth survey of specific artists. Tour reservations necessary. Free street parking. The gift shop has a very interesting array of contemporary jewelry, unusual high-tech gifts, stationery, prints, books, and contemporary monographs. Picnic area. Wheelchair access, parking and elevator.

Open Tuesday, Thursday-Sunday 10 A.M.-5 P.M., Wednesday 10 A.M.-9 P.M. Closed Mondays. Admission is $2 for adults, 50¢ for children under 12, senior citizens and students $1. No charge on Wednesdays. For more information call (619) 454-3541 or (619) 454-0267.

Mingci International Museum of World Folk Art
University Towne Center, San Diego, CA 92122

GETTING THERE: From either the San Diego Fwy (I-5) or the Inland Fwy (I-805), take the La Jolla Village Dr. exit. The museum is located at La Jolla Village Dr. and Genesee.

Unique in its location, this museum is situated in a large shopping center called the University Towne Center. Attracting many shoppers to its contemporary gallery, the museum focuses on folk art of India, Mexico, Japan, and Nepal. Objects from other countries are also displayed in the stark white gallery, which highlights the vibrant colors of cultural arts. Frequently complementing an exhibit theme is the presence of work-in-progress by international folk artists. Guided tours every Thursday at 1:30 P.M. The gift shop sells a wide range of folk art pieces from many countries. Several restaurants inside the shopping mall. Free parking. Wheelchair access and parking.

Open Tuesday–Thursday and Saturday 11 A.M.–5 P.M., Friday until 9 P.M., Sunday 2–5 P.M. Closed Mondays. Suggested donation of $2. For more information call (619) 453-5300.

Mission San Diego de Alcala
10818 San Diego Mission Road, San Diego, CA 92108

GETTING THERE: Take Mission Valley Fwy (I-8) to Mission Gorge Road. Go north to Twain Ave., turn left. It becomes San Diego Mission Road after one block.

Known as Mother of the Missions, this was the first of a chain of twenty-one missions established along the California coast. One year after its construction in 1774, an Indian raid destroyed it, and the second structure was damaged by an earthquake. This building has withstood successive earthquakes, and serves today as an active parish and cultural center.

Southwest Indian pottery, basketry, and costumes, and an interesting photographic display of the mission from its ruin to restoration are well worth seeing. In addition are archaeological findings. Showing only a small part of its holdings, the mission has plans to build a larger museum facility.

Annual events include Fiesta of the Bells and Blessing of the Animals in July. The gift shops sells religious items and books on California history. Wheelchair access. No restaurant. Free parking. Tours for ten or more may be reserved two weeks in advance. A self-guided "Tout-a-Tape" is available.

Open daily 8 A.M.–5 P.M. Admission is $1 for adults, 50¢ for children. For more information call (619) 283-7319 and (619) 281-8449.

Mission San Diego de Alcala, the first California mission. Photo by Sara LeBien.

Museum of Photographic Arts
1649 El Prado, Balboa Park, San Diego, CA 92101

GETTING THERE: From Cabrillo Fwy (163) take the Laurel St. exit east into park. From San Diego Fwy (I-5) take the Park Blvd. exit north into park. Follow signs.

A new photographic art exhibit opens every six to eight weeks at this museum. Only a handful of museums in America are devoted exclusively to photographic art, and this one was the first. Dedicated to human expression as seen through photography, film, and video, the exhibits span the history of photography, motion pictures, and video, displaying everything from nineteenth-century daguerreotypes to the latest in computer-controlled imagery, video art, and laser scan. One temporary show, "Masters of the Street," presented a contemporary vision of street genre, first featuring works by Henri Cartier-Bresson, Robert Frank, Josef Koudelka, Gary Winogrand, and William Klein followed later by Ernesto Bazan, Anthony Hernandez, Raghubir Singh, and others. Other major shows highlighted the work of Edward Weston and Hiroshima photography by Hiromi Tsuchida.

Housed in the famous Casa de Balboa in Balboa Park, the museum's spaciousness and simplicity create a fine setting for the display of photographic arts. Its video installations, using the most contemporary film technology, add another dimension to the museum's philosophy of informing and stimulating its viewers in the new forms of art expression. Special programs include films, lectures, workshops, and annual events such as the annual awards exhibition, a competition open to amateurs and professionals. Educational services available are the ongoing lecture series, workshops, extension collaborative programs with schools, and a community outreach program. Free parking. Docent tours by reservation only. The gift shop offers an excellent selection of books. A large cafe in Casa de Balboa, and other restaurants and picnic areas are also located in the park. Wheelchair access and parking.

Open daily 10 A.M.–5 P.M., Thursdays until 9 P.M. Admission is $2 for adults, children under 12 free, $2 for senior citizens. For more information call (619) 239-5262.

Old Town San Diego State Historic Park

San Diego Ave. and Mason St., San Diego, CA 92211

GETTING THERE: Take Mission Valley/Ocean Beach Fwy (I–8) to Taylor exit. Go south. Follow signs to Old Town.

Old Town is the original city, inhabited by the early settlers who were an extension of the mission. Through the years it has grown through the addition of shops and restaurants for tourists, but in 1968 the original section became a state historic park and was restored to recreate the early Mexican and American periods of its past. At the center of Old Town between Wallace and Twiggs streets and Juan and Congress streets, is the genuine *old* town, where visitors will find the historic structures. Some of them are now museums. The visitors center is a good place to get an overview of the area and obtain a very helpful tour-guide booklet. Lectures, films, craft demonstrations. A slide program about San Diego's early history is given at the Seeley Stable three times a day. Restaurant. Wheelchair access in most areas. Free parking lots throughout Old Town.

There are ten historic homes throughout Old Town that are well worth a visit: Casa de Estudillo (1829); Casa de Machado y Stewart (1829); Mason Street School (1865); San Diego Union Building (1851); Casa de Machado y Silvas (1830); Casa de Bandini (1829); Seeley Stables (1869); Casa de Rodriguez (Racine & Laramie Store) (1869); La Casa de Pedrorena (1869); San Diego Union Building (1868).

Open daily 10 A.M.–5 P.M. in winter. Summer hours are 10 A.M.–6 P.M. Entrance fees are charged at La Casa de Estudillo and the Seeley Stable; a ticket purchased at either is good for both on the same day and also for a slide show at the Seeley Stable. For more information call (619) 237-6770.

Reuben H. Fleet Space Theater and Science Center

El Prado, Balboa Park, San Diego, CA 92103

GETTING THERE: From Cabrillo Fwy (163) take the Laurel St. exit east into park. From San Diego Fwy (I–5) take the Park Blvd. exit north into park. Follow signs.

A 9,500-square-foot exhibition area is filled with more than fifty participatory science exhibits, each one demonstrating natural

San Diego Union, one of the first frame houses in Historic Old Town San Diego. Photo by Sara LeBien.

phenomena and providing interaction with a particular science principle. Visitors can observe gravitational forces in action at a "gravity well," measure the time it takes their own bodies to recognize and react to a signal in a participatory exhibit on the reflex system, and learn about the properties of surface tension in a special exhibit that uses soap bubbles. Using polarized light, a bone-stress exhibit shows the lines of stress that occur in a plastic model of a thigh bone when put under pressure. A submarine periscope that goes through the roof is also fun to try.

The museum's space theater offers state-of-the-art film production. Omnimax, with its massive picture projected onto a tilted seventy-six-foot dome, creates unprecedented realism in films about the solar system, Mt. St. Helens, and a space shuttle voyage. The museum hosts seminars, lectures, a summer space program, and workshops in astronomy, space exploration, the human body, physics, illusions, and other subjects. Laserium light shows and Omnimax films are presented daily. Call for show times and ticket prices. Annual events include National Space Week, second week in July. With programs for school groups designed to meet curriculum framework for San Diego schools, the center provides teachers' guides, tours, and film shows.

The cafes in Museum of Art Sculpture Garden and Casa de Balboa both have a pleasant ambiance. Picnic area outside. A wonderful assortment of science games, gifts, toys, puzzles, compasses, and books are in the gift shop.

Open Sunday–Thursday 9:45 A.M.–9:30 P.M., Friday and Saturday 9:45 A.M.–10:30 P.M. Admission for adults is $4.50, $2.75 for children 15 and under, $3 for senior citizens. Admission includes one theater show as well. Groups of 25 or more with advance reservations receive a 20 percent discount on admissions. Free parking. For more information call (619) 238-1168 or (619) 238-1233.

San Diego Aerospace Museum
2001 Pan American Plaza, Balboa Park, San Diego, CA 92101

GETTING THERE: From Cabrillo Fwy (163) take the Laurel St. exit east into park. From San Diego Fwy (I-5) take the Park Blvd. exit north into park. Follow signs.

Claiming to be second only to the Smithsonian in its aviation collection, this outstanding museum presents innovative and

The San Diego Aerospace Museum claims the best aviation collection in the West. Photo by Sara LeBien.

beautiful displays exploring the history of aviation from its beginning to the space age. It is hard to believe that in 1978 this museum collection of aircraft was totally destroyed in a fire. The assistance and dedication of aviation experts and a large volunteer force have since then completely reproduced the seventy-two aircraft.

Featured at the entrance is a grand tribute to Charles Lindbergh. Other San Diego aviation pioneers are honored along with Reuben H. Fleet who inaugurated the first U.S. Airmail service in 1918. A realistic recreation shows the mail plane being unloaded and the waiting Model T delivery truck, while an audio presentation lets visitors hear the conversation of the mail employees as they work. The wall behind them displays giant size historical airmail stamps.

In the Aerospace Hall of Fame visitors can view moon rocks, lunar samples collected by astronauts on Apollo 17, and portraits of aeronautical notables in the military, aerospace industry, and space program. Beautiful murals from the 1935 California-Pacific Expo in 1935 called *The March of Transportation*, and covering a space 18 by 468 feet long, make up the largest mural in the U.S.

Special programs include films and model workshops with a Master Modeler. Annual events include a model contest each fall and aviation art shows. Historical aviation library of 6,000 volumes of vintage aeronautical books, magazines, manuals, documents, and photographs. Free parking. Gift shop sells aviation books, prints, models, and apparel. Wheelchair access and parking.

Open daily 10 A.M.–4:40 P.M. Closed Thanksgiving, Christmas, and New Year's Day. Admission is $3.50 for adults, $1 for children, senior citizens free on first Tuesday of each month. For more information call (619) 234 8291.

San Diego Hall of Champions
1649 El Prado, Balboa Park, San Diego, CA 92112

GETTING THERE: From Cabrillo Fwy (163) take the Laurel St. exit east into park. From San Diego Fwy (I–5) take the Park Blvd. exit north into park. Follow signs.

The visually striking colorful exhibits at this museum feature forty sports events, including San Diego's own "Over-the-Line," a version of softball played on the local beaches, which is explained here

The ornate Casa de Balboa houses the San Diego Hall of Champions, as well as the Museum of Photographic Arts and the Model Railroad Museum. Photo by Sara LeBien.

in video and miniature display. Military athletes and disabled champions are given recognition, as well as those honored in the Breitbard Hall of Fame, a focal point in the center of the exhibition hall. These honorees are either former or current residents of San Diego or have played in San Diego while achieving national and international acclaim. Some of those champions honored are famed baseball hitter Ted Williams, swimmer Florence Chadwick, boxer Archie Moore, tennis champion Maureen Connelly, and sailor Dennis Conner. Museum features collections and displays of sports equipment, memorabilia, medals, and trophies. Bill Muncey's sleek Atlas Van Lines U–71 racing boat is also here. There is also a photo essay on the Special Olympics, highlighted by its slogan, "Let me win, but if I cannot win, let me be brave in the attempt." The museum offers educational seminars, workshops, and films. Film theatre runs sports films continuously. Annual events include a "Salute to the Champions" awards dinner and a "Christmas on the Prado" open house. Two cafes and picnic area on premises. Free parking. The gift shop sells a wide assortment of sports-related souvenirs, badges, pins, clothing, and gifts. Wheelchair access and parking.

Open Monday–Saturday 10 A.M.–4:30 P.M. and Sunday noon–5 P.M. Admission is $2 for adults, 50¢ for children, senior citizens $1. For more information call (619) 234-2544.

San Diego Model Railroad Museum
Casa de Balboa Building, 1649 El Prado, San Diego, CA 92101

GETTING THERE: From Cabrillo Fwy (163) take the Laurel St. exit east into park. From San Diego Fwy (I-5) take the Park Blvd. exit north into park. Follow signs. Casa de Balboa is located on El Prado across from the San Diego Museum of Art and the Timken Gallery.

In the lower level of the Casa de Balboa Building is an elaborate model railroad museum. Accurate, cleverly detailed railroad scenes are assembled by various model railroad clubs for public viewing. One example is the Southern Pacific-Santa Fe Tehachapi Pass HO (¹/₈₇ actual size) Scale Exhibit. Leaving Bakersfield yards, trains roll down the San Joaquin Valley to the Caliente Creek narrows, where the steep grade begins. The journey continues through the mountains, past the famous Tehachapi Loop where in actuality the rail system begins a great spiral loop. Twelve feet

109

above floor level trains peak Tehachapi summit and race down into the Mojave Desert. Three other model railroad landscapes constructions are Cabrillo Southwestern O Scale, Pacific Desert Lines N Scale, and San Diego and Arizona Eastern HO Scale. Lectures and newsletter available. Educational services include work sessions Tuesday–Friday 7:30–11 P.M. Gift shop sells railroad books, toys, crafts, and gifts. Two cafes on premises. Free parking. Wheelchair access.

Open Friday 11 A.M.–4 P.M., Saturday and Sunday 11 A.M.–5 P.M. Admission is $1 for adults, children free. For more information call (619) 696-0199.

San Diego Museum of Art
El Prado, Balboa Park, San Diego, CA 92112–2107

GETTING THERE: From Cabrillo Fwy (163) take the Laurel St. exit east into park. From San Diego Fwy (I–5) take the Park Blvd. exit north into park. Follow signs.

The museum's ornate Spanish Baroque entrance, in likeness to the hammered silver of Spain and a section of the University of Salamanca in Spain, establishes the setting for its collection of Italian renaissance, Dutch and Spanish baroque, Asian art, nineteenth-century European paintings, and twentieth-century painting and sculpture, decorative arts, and Indian and Persian miniatures. More museum holdings include works by Giorgione, Titan, Van Dyck, Frans Hals, Rembrandt, Murillo, Zurbarán, El Greco, Goya, Rubens, Thomas Lawrence, and Joshua Reynolds. In addition is a comprehensive collection of American art. Besides its permanent collection of ten thousand significant works of art from Egyptian and pre-Columbian to the twentieth century, the museum displays up to six major international art exhibitions each year as well as a number of smaller shows.

There are Wednesday morning hands-on workshops on color, creative solutions to problems, landscape sketching, and sculpture. Saturday studio classes are offered to children and adults. Friday morning lecture series. Also "Meet the Masters" lecture-luncheon series, slide talks, and more.

Docents present art programs at schools prior to the students' museum trip. Guided tour provides behind-the-scenes look at

With an outer façade reminiscent of the University of Salamanca, the San Diego Museum of Art houses unparalleled treasures for the San Diego area. Courtesy of museum.

museum activity. Workshops for school groups. Regular docent tours are offered in the galleries Tuesday–Thursday 10 A.M., 11 A.M., 1 P.M., and also at 1 P.M. on Sunday. Other tours can be scheduled by calling (619) 232-7931. With a strong emphasis on education, the museum has developed a program of classes for children and adults in cooperation with local schools and universities. In conjunction with the permanent and special exhibitions there are lectures, seminars, and film programs. "Art to Art" is a guided tour emphasizing conceptual and visual connections to concurrent Shakespeare productions at the nearby Old Globe theater. May S. March Sculpture Court, a 450-seat James S. Copley Auditorium, and a reference library of 13,000 volumes, 40,000 exhibition catalogs, and 16,000 slides. Annual junior art activity day.

The gift shop offers a large selection of art books, art magazines, prints, cards, videos, and cassettes on Degas, Chagall, O'Keefe, and others. Two cafes nearby, also vendor and picnic area outside. Free parking. Wheelchair access and parking.

Open Tuesday–Sunday 10 A.M.–4:30 P.M. Admission is $4 for adults, $2 for children, students with ID, and senior citizens. For more information call (619) 232-7931.

San Diego Museum of Man
1350 El Prado Blvd., Balboa Park, San Diego, CA 92101

GETTING THERE: From Cabrillo Fwy (163) take the Laurel St. exit east into park. From San Diego Fwy (I–5) take the Park Blvd. exit north into park. Follow signs.

Dedicated to fostering an understanding of anthropology, this museum was founded during the 1915 Panama-California Exposition, and focuses on learning cultural and ethnic origins. This is reflected in the permanent exhibitions that explain the process of human evolution and the cultures of early man, followed later by Indian tribes, and the interrelationships between man and animals. Elaborate dioramas of physical and cultural differentiation contain full-scale models of early man. Vibrant settings show artifacts, art, costumes, textiles, and photographs demonstrating the progression of man's development. On weekends volunteers demonstrate their skills at traditional weaving, spinning, and preparing food.

Zapotec weaver Gabino Jiminez demonstrates his skill at weaving. Courtesy of San Diego Museum of Man.

The museum also displays historical Mayan artifacts; pueblo pottery; artifacts from the coastal, desert, and mountain environments of the Kumeyaay Indians, the early inhabitants of the San Diego area; artifacts from the Plains, Southwest, and Pacific Northwest Coast; and Hopi artifacts such as textiles, ceramics, basketry, woodcarving, jewelry, and Kachina dolls. Films, lectures, workshops. Annual events include the Haunted Museum (October 25–31), Indian Fair (second weekend in June), and Rock Art Symposium (first weekend in November).

The library of over 13,000 books and seventy-two archival manuscripts and periodicals on anthropology, archaeology, ethnology is available for interlibrary loan and for scholars, teachers, and graduate students. An extensive education program planned with the school's curriculum offers tours, demonstrations, classroom presentations, films, and classes for in-depth study of anthropology. Tour reservations must be made at least six weeks in advance. Tours are free for schools but charge $1 per adult and 10¢ per child for other groups. The advance reservation is to allow time for a packet of information about the exhibits to be sent to you. For more details call the museum. A fine bookstore and gift shop sells Indian jewelry, textiles, and folk art. Also a large selection of books on Native Americans. Picnic area in nearby park. Wheelchair access. Free parking.

Open daily 10 A.M.–4:30 P.M. Admission is $2 for adults, 25¢ for children 6–16, 50¢ for students. For more information call (619) 239-2001.

San Diego Natural History Museum
Balboa Park, San Diego, CA 92112

GETTING THERE: From Cabrillo Fwy (163) take the Laurel St. exit east into park. From San Diego Fwy (I–5) take the Park Blvd. exit north into park. Follow signs.

This museum's exhibits focus on plants, animals, and geology of San Diego County. Exhibitions reconstruct the natural scenes of the regional plants and animals. There is a seashore recreation where a thirty-foot gray whale skeleton is partially buried in sand, and visitors can see a whale skull over sixteen feet long. The interior skeleton of a recreated dolphin is exposed, and an audio presentation tells the warning signs of a rattlesnake strike.

Displays include a Foucault Pendulum showing the daily rotation of the earth on its axis, and a seismograph recording movements of the earth's crust. The museum has an extensive permanent collection of shells, insects, mammals, birds, invertebrates, reptiles, amphibians, plant and animal fossils, minerals, and gems. Reservations required for tours. Special programs include nature outings and weekend field trips led by qualified naturalists, natural history films shown on weekends in auditorium, lectures, workshops, free canyon walk each Sunday at 2 P.M. in Balboa Park. Hands-on exhibits on Saturdays. Docent community programs available for convalescent homes, special groups. "C–4–U" nature walks (one-on-one docent tours with visually impaired visitors.) Annual events include weekend boat trips in January to see migrating whales.

Educational services offered include tours for different age groups, lectures, films, study classes, TV and radio programs for adults and children, mobile vans, exhibit-loan library for school loan, tactile mobile museum for blind, deaf, and physically handicapped, K–3 workshops, age three-to-adult canyon tours, classroom programs for grades 3-6. There is an 80,000 volume library on natural history available for interlibrary loan and to students with appointment and to institutions. Also a 300-seat auditorium, nature center, and classrooms. Gift shop offers minerals, shells, books, and many dinosaur books and gifts. Picnic area with wheelchair access.

Open daily 10 A.M.–4:30 P.M. Closed Thanksgiving, Christmas, and New Year's Day. Admission is $4.00 for those over 12, $1.00 for 12 and under. Free parking. For more information call (619) 232-3821.

San Diego Zoo
Balboa Park, San Diego, CA 92112-0551

GETTING THERE: From Cabrillo Fwy (163) take the Laurel St. exit east into park. From San Diego Fwy (I-5) take the Park Blvd. exit north into park. Follow signs.

The world famous San Diego Zoo will have over three million visitors this year. The one hundred-acre tropical garden-site houses 32,000 animals of 800 species, including rare and exotic species. Such notables are wild Przewalski's horses from Mongolia, pygmy chimps from central Africa, and a New Guinea tree crocodile. The zoo's collection of *psittacine* (parrots and parrot-like) is the largest ever assembled.

A unique viewing experience is to ride the third-of-a-mile Skyfari which skims treetops and traverses the ape grottos, sea lion pool, and other exhibits. The Children's Zoo has spider monkeys, river otters, and walk-through bird cages. Also a hands-on area with gentle animals, and an incubator showing egg-hatching. The fascinating, glass-enclosed nursery reveals infant primates and mammals being bottle-fed and diapered.

Educational programs range from kindergarten through college. Summer zoology classes are offered for grades 3–12 and adults. A three-hour tour on private bus is $16.50 for adults and $9.50 for children and students. Two-hour tour is $14.50 for adults and $7.50 for children. Special tours for special groups, including blind or deaf.

Custom tours also available for groups. All tours by advance reservation only. Times are flexible. Call (619) 231–1515 or write to P.O. Box 551, San Diego, CA 92112–0551. Free animal shows daily. Stroller and wheelchair rental. Restaurants and deli. Special group facilities. Gift shops and camera shops.

Labor Day through June: 9 A.M.–4 P.M. July through Labor Day: 9 A.M.–5 P.M. Admission is $7.50 for adults, $2.50 for ages 3–15, age 2 and under free. Children's Zoo: 50¢ for age 3 and above, age 2 and under free. Skyfari (one way), $1 for adults, 75¢ for ages 3–15, age 2 and under free. For more information call (619) 234–3153 or (619) 231–1515.

Scripps Aquarium/Museum
8602 La Jolla Shores Dr., La Jolla, CA 92093

GETTING THERE: Take the San Diego Fwy (I–5) to Ardath Road. Go west to La Jolla Shores Dr. Turn right and follow to Scripps Institution of Oceanography. Follow signs to aquarium/museum.

Since 1903 the San Diego Marine Biological Association, while conducting biological and hydrographic surveys of the waters of the California Pacific Ocean, has maintained a public aquarium and museum.

At the entrance to the aquarium is a tide pool which attracts many curious spectators, and inside are fine exhibits explaining deep sea exploration, world climate, and the greenhouse effect. Another demonstrates a wave channel, and El Niño, the warming trend, is explained. One exhibition shows the structure of the earth's crusts and how the sea floor is spreading and changing the position of the continents, supporting the theory of continental drift. A deep-sea instrument capsule and exhibits on oceanographic research are also fascinating. In addition, visitors may walk along a series of large tanks displaying a wide variety of fish, and invertebrates including seahorses, turtles, starfish, and moray eels. Lectures and films. Metered parking. No restaurant. Wheelchair access and parking.

Open daily 9 A.M.–5 P.M. including holidays. Admission is free but donations are appreciated. For a recorded message call (619) 534-6933 or for more information call (619) 534-4086.

Sea World

1720 South Shores Road, Mission Bay, San Diego, CA 92109

GETTING THERE: From the San Diego Fwy (I-5) exit west onto Sea World Dr. Or follow Ocean Beach Fwy (I-8) onto West Mission Bay Dr. and continue east to Sea World.

The public may think of Sea World only as a tourist attraction for marine entertainment, but Sea World also has a fine reputation for marine life exhibits. Many recreated natural settings, including an Antarctic exhibit with its penguin chick nursery, are highly entertaining, and exhibits such as the dolphin petting pool fascinate visitors of all ages. Guided tours, narrations, educational materials, photographs, and scale models all are thoughtfully designed to assure that visitors leave with a better understanding and appreciation of marine life.

Sea World has thirty educational exhibits on all phases of marine life, twenty-five aquarium displays, twenty-five displays featuring freshwater fish, four 55,000 gallon pools featuring large kelp-bed fish, a coral reef, schooling fish, game fish, tidepool exhibit, walrus, aviary and penguin exhibit. Ten major education programs for preschool through college levels are offered on site and through visiting docent programs. They include slides, puppet shows,

117

marine specimens, and live animal shows. Audio-visual outreach program. Through a special telephone hook-up, classes can participate in a question-and-answer session with a Sea World instructor.

Ninety-minute guided tour available offered every thirty minutes from 9 A.M.–2 P.M. Cost of tour is $3 for adults, $2 for children. Classes for all ages and free resources for teachers also are offered. Several restaurants. Wheelchair access. Stroller and wheelchair rentals.

Open daily 9 A.M. to dusk. Admission is $19.95 for adults, $14.95 for ages 3–11, under 3 free. Credit cards accepted. For more information call (619) 222-6363.

Junipero Serra Museum
2727 Presidio Dr., San Diego, CA 92103

GETTING THERE: Take Ocean Beach Fwy I–8 to the Taylor St. exit, go south, and follow signs to Presidio Park. It is near Old Town.

A significant historical site, comparable to the establishment of Jamestown and Plymouth in the East, this was the first established community on the Pacific coast by the Spanish Empire. Father Junipero Serra, the Spanish missionary who accompanied the first Spanish expedition to California, built the first mission within the Spanish Presidio. Named Mission San Diego de Alcala, it was here from 1769 until 1774 when it was relocated six miles away. None of those original buildings remain, but this structure was built in 1929 to display remaining artifacts and to honor Father Serra.

The Spanish-style building has displays of a pre-Anglo era when San Diego was first colonized. Artifacts from Presidio excavations, such as hand-forged tools and hardware, ceramic fragments, and a large olive press and grinding stones represent daily mission life. The grass-covered mounds throughout the Presidio grounds are slated for further excavation. The main exhibition hall, with its high ceiling and massive beams, displays furniture in a beautiful room setting, part of the finest collection of seventeenth-century Spanish renaissance furniture in the West. Rancho and mission period items comprise other displays, and one room is devoted to colorful objects from Mallorca, Spain, the birthplace of Father Serra. Visitors can climb up into the tower where changing exhibits are located, and from which there is a panoramic view of the Mission Valley, Mission Bay, and the Pacific Ocean.

Open Monday–Saturday 9 A.M.–4:45 P.M. and Sunday noon–4:45 P.M. Admission is $1 for adults, children under 12 free. For more information call (619) 297-3258.

Star of India—Maritime Museum Association of San Diego

1306 Harbor Dr., San Diego, CA 92101

GETTING THERE: Take San Diego Fwy (I-5) to Front St. exit. Turn south on Front, west onto Ash St., and follow to the waterfront.

Three world-famous ships are moored next to each other, two of which have fine nautical exhibitions and additional displays about the development of San Diego Bay. The *Star of India,* the oldest iron-hulled ship afloat, is a full-rigged merchant ship built in 1893. Used to haul cargo and transport immigrants from London to New Zealand, her rig was changed to a "bark" (square sails on her foremast and mainmast) for greater maneuverability in 1901 when she was purchased by the Alaska salmon industry. She has been in San Diego since 1926 and was sailed on 4 July 1976 to honor the Bicentennial. On display is a collection of humorous ships-in-bottles and an exhibit explaining how this is accomplished. Also on view is the former crew's living quarters with personal items from their long voyages. In addition is a photo exhibit of the Bicentennial excursion.

Built in 1898, the *Berkeley* was a ferryboat, transporting passengers and commuters between terminals in San Francisco and Oakland. She participated in the evacuation of San Francisco following the 1906 earthquake, when ferries ran for twenty-four hours a day carrying thousands of refugees to Oakland. On view below deck is a collection of beautiful ship models and other nautical exhibits. Visitors can see the model restoration shop where repairs and maintenance on the collection is done and where professional model builders put in 5,000 to 10,000 hours on one intricate model after researching historical plans and photos for accuracy.

Additional facilities include a nautical research library open for accredited students by prior arrangement. Films and lectures.

The Star of India's *only cargo now is the story of her life. Photo by Sara LeBien.*

Educational services include speakers bureau, scheduled tours, classroom visits. Restaurants, coffee shops, and picnic areas are nearby. Wheelchair access only on the *Berkeley*. Gift shop features books, nautical brass gifts, prints, posters, ship models, reproductions of scrimshaw.

Open daily 9 A.M.–8 P.M. Admission is $4 for adults, $1 for children 6–12, $3 for 13–17, $3 for senior citizens, $8 per family. Metered street parking. Scheduled tours for groups must be made two weeks in advance, but docents sometimes conduct impromptu tours for a few visitors. For more information call (619) 234-9153.

Timken Art Gallery
1500 El Prado, Balboa Park, San Diego, CA 92101

GETTING THERE: From Cabrillo Fwy (163) take the Laurel St. exit east into park. From San Diego Fwy (I–5) take the Park Blvd. exit north into park. Follow signs.

Formerly displaying their works of art in the Fine Arts Gallery, before it became the San Diego Museum of Art, the Timken family later provided a new building to house its growing collection of European and American paintings, Gobelin tapestries, and Russian icons. The gallery's rotunda houses a bronze replica of Mercury surrounded by four exquisite tapestries. Adjoining galleries display paintings and Russian icons. Represented in the European gallery are artists Boucher, Pieter Bruegel the Elder, Cagnacci, Cezanne, Corot, Frans Hals, Rubens, and Rembrandt. Some American artists on view are Bierstadt, Cropsey, Innes, and Benjamin West. Icons, the single panels or complex combinations of panels, have colorful religious scenes and were used for Russian Orthodox devotions in private homes and in churches. Icons on display here include single panels that represent individual apostles, and more elaborate pieces depicting full scenes with many figures and religious symbols.

"Painting of the Week" lectures are offered on most Wednesdays at 1:30 P.M. Docent tours are available Tuesday and Thursday between 10 A.M. and noon. Special tours for groups require a ten-day advance notice. Good selection of art books, cards, and some reproductions in gift shop. Two cafes across from the gallery, picnic area nearby. Wheelchair access. Free parking near the gallery.

Open Tuesday–Saturday 10 A.M.–4:30 P.M. and Sunday 1:30–4:30 P.M. Closed throughout September and on New Year's Day, 4th of July, Thanksgiving, and Christmas. Free admission. For more information call (619) 239-5548.

Villa Montezuma/Jesse Shepard House

1925 K St., San Diego, CA 92102

GETTING THERE: Go south on San Diego Fwy (I-5) to the Imperial Ave. exit. Go east on Imperial to 20th St., north to K St.

In 1889 the *San Diego Sun* described Jesse Shepard's house as "the most ornately finished and artistically furnished house in the city . . . itself a museum." Nearly a hundred years later it is an outstanding example of eclectic Victorian and Queen Anne design. Restored by the San Diego Historical Society, it is the city's finest Victorian landmark and reflects the opulent life-style during the 1886–1888 oil boom.

Jesse Shepard was an internationally known author and musician. Before settling in San Diego he had traveled throughout Europe performing for nobility. This house was designed to reflect his artistic interests and provide a setting for concerts and lavish musical galas. The music room and conservatory are embellished with stained-glass windows of Beethoven and Mozart. Other art glass depicts Greek mythology, Corneille, Shakespeare, and Goethe. The many rooms are named with the color used in each decor. The Gold Room is a library of beautifully bound books on art, literature, and music. The Pink Room has lovely art glass windows designed with grapes and floral motifs. The museum on the second floor displays works of art, decorative arts, and memorabilia from Shepard's travels. Spanish cedar stairs lead up to the observatory, which offers a panoramic view of the city. There are twelve areas in which to view furnishings, costumes, magnificent stained glass, and beautiful wall paneling and hardwood floors. The second-floor gallery has changing exhibits of costumes, and Victorian furnishings.

Shepard's villa still serves as a community cultural center. In keeping with the original use of the home, it is often the setting for musical presentations and poetry readings. Films and lectures, musical festivals, chamber music concerts, poetry readings. Annual events include the villa's spectacular Christmas

The Villa Montezuma/Jesse Shepard House is a wonderful example of Victorian design. Courtesy of museum.

decorations and participation in America's Finest City Week each August. Outreach program with city schools. Tour reservations are only required for groups. Picnic area. Books, handcrafted and quilted items, and other museum-related items are for sale in museum shop. Street parking.

Open daily Tuesday–Friday and Sunday 1–4 P.M. Admission is $2 for adults, children under 12 free, $2 for senior citizens. For more information call (619) 239-2211.

Chapter Seven

Riverside and San Bernardino Counties

California Museum of Photography
University of California, Riverside, CA 92521

GETTING THERE: Take the Pomona Fwy (60) to University Ave. in Riverside. Go east two blocks to the end of the street, turn left to the first building. In Fall 1988 please call for directions to the new location.

Although affiliated with the university, this museum is oriented toward the general public. Both permanent and changing exhibitions draw from its extensive collection of 10,000 photographs, 12,000 cameras and photographic accessories, and over 350,000 stereographs. The print collection represents a broad range of work, both early and modern, of major photographers such as Adam Clark, Vroman, Edward Curtis, Ansel Adams, Albert Renger-Patzsch, Edward Weston, and Berenice Abott. Also included are works made in 1846 by Anna Atkins, who is considered to be the first female photographer. Other works represent members of the "f/64" movement of photography that celebrated landscape imagery of the American West from the 1920s to the 1950s. One of these was Walker Evans who documented the Depression Years. Strong in its representation of western landscape photography, the museum houses 6,000 negatives and 600 photographs by Ansel Adams. Barbara Morgan's images of the art of dance comprise another extensive collection.

The museum offers workshops, films, lectures, and family-oriented activities. Discovery kits on photography are available for schools, as well as special tours for school groups. It is known in the photography world not only for its collections but for a humanities-oriented approach to photography. After moving in

Clearing Winter Storm, Yosemite National Park, *1944. Ansel Adams.*
Courtesy of the California Museum of Photography, University of
California–Riverside.

Fall 1988, the museum will find a new home in the 1929 Kress variety store. Its extensive renovation by noted San Francisco artist and architect Stanley Saitowitz provides 10,000 square feet of exhibition galleries and 2,400 square feet for workshops and special events. Annual event is the Photographers' Christmas Card exhibit and open house.

Permanent collection includes the Keystone-Mast Collection of over 350,000 stereoscopic negatives from 1892 to the 1930s, the Zeiss Collection of 8,000 cameras, the Bingham Collection representing cameras of all periods of photographic history, and a collection of 12,000 photographs by pioneering and contemporary art photographers. There is a gift shop and restaurant, free parking, and wheelchair access. Free admission.

Open Tuesday–Saturday 10 A.M.–5 P.M., Sunday noon–5 P.M. Closed Mondays. (Hours and admission may change at the new building.) For current information and tour reservations call (714) 787–4787 or (714) 784–FOTO for a recorded message.

Casa de Rancho Cucamonga—The Rains Museum
Hemlock and Vineyard, Rancho Cucamonga, CA 91730

GETTING THERE: From Los Angeles, drive east on the San Bernardino Fwy (I–10) past Ontario-Upland to the Vineyard Ave. exit. Go north about 2½ miles to Foothill Blvd. Continue two blocks north on Vineyard to Hemlock.

Shoshone Indians were the first settlers in the *Kukumonga* village. The land later became part of the holdings of the rich San Gabriel Mission. Saved from demolition in 1971, the house now serves as a museum of local history with eight rooms furnished in the period between 1860 and 1880 including, among many items, a square piano, an 1870 globe chandelier of beautiful handpainted roses, and two rope beds. The tar that seals the roof was brought in by cart all the way from the La Brea tar pits. There are temporary shows of artifacts from the Shoshone Indians, Chinatown, and local history. Annual events include Old Rancho Day in May, and a gourmet Christmas dinner. Conducted tours, reservations required for ten or more. Call (714) 985–5329. Special tours available for school classes. Picnic area, wheelchair access.

Open Wednesday–Sunday noon–4 P.M. Closed Mondays and Tuesdays. Free admission and parking. For more information call (714) 989–4970.

Edward-Dean Museum of Decorative Arts
9401 Oak Glen Road, Cherry Valley, CA 92233

GETTING THERE: From San Bernardino Fwy (I–10) take Cherry Valley Blvd. exit east to Beaumont Ave. Head north to museum road sign, go left. From Pomona Fwy (60), which joins I–10, take Beaumont Ave. exit north approximately six miles to museum road sign.

J. Edward Eberic and Dean W. Stout were partners in an antiques and decorating business on La Cienega Boulevard in Los Angeles. One had an eye for antiques and the other knew how to display them. Housed in a handsome, Italian-style villa and entry garden, this museum is a result of their years of collecting decorative arts from many eras. Viewing the collections is like touring an opulent historic home, filled with the eclectic and beautiful, spanning the seventeenth through nineteenth centuries. On display are furnishings, paintings, bronzes, paperweights, ceramics, and a highly esteemed collection of eighteenth- and nineteenth-century Tibetan and Chinese gilded bronzes. Other collections include decorative arts of European and Asian textiles, fans, ivory and jade carvings, David Roberts watercolors, European paintings, Meissen porcelain. Cloisonne collection includes incense burners, vases, and an incense clock. Carved panelings by Grinling Gibbons, one of the most skillful woodcarvers ever known, are here. A unique educational program has been developed for all age groups with emphasis on creativity and art appreciation. Films, lectures, workshops. Outdoor pavilion available for seminars, receptions, and special events. Reservations required for tours. Picnic area available by reservation. Wheelchair access and parking.

Open Tuesday–Friday 1–4:30 P.M. and 10 A.M.–4:30 P.M. on weekends. Closed Mondays. Admission is $1 for adults, children under 12 free. For more information call (714) 845–2626.

Fontana Farms Camp #1 Museum
8863 Pepper St., Fontana, CA 92335

GETTING THERE: From the San Bernardino Fwy (I–10), take the Sierra Ave. exit. Drive north three miles on Sierra, turn left onto Merrill Ave., go ½ mile, then right onto Pepper Ave.

This museum is a farm frozen in time with a farmhouse, bunkhouse, and blacksmith shop remaining just as they were in the late 1800s. House furnishings, original tools, and farming equipment are the main displays. One room in the bunkhouse is furnished for the hired help.

Education programs include special tours for school children and lectures by museum staff in schools. The museum also has a research library located at 8459 Wheeler Street which is open on Mondays 1–4 P.M. Call (714) 823-1773 for library reservations. Films, lectures and workshops. Participation in annual city celebrations and Christmas party for children. Books and postcards are for sale. No restaurant. Free parking, wheelchair access.

Open Saturdays only, 1–4 P.M. Free admission. For tour reservations and more information call (714) 823-3846.

Heritage House

8193 Magnolia Ave., Riverside, CA 92504

GETTING THERE: Take Riverside Fwy (91) to Adams St. exit. Go west to Magnolia Ave., turn north, and then right to the mansion.

Considered to be one of the best restored and furnished historical houses in the state, this elaborate Victorian mansion was once a predominant feature on Magnolia Avenue in the affluent orange-growing region of Riverside in the 1890s. The complex exterior has a domed tower with Moorish fretwork framing the windows, and elaborate details such as recessed porches and lavishly carved oak woodwork grace the mansion. Original furniture, interior shutters, and oriental rugs lend themselves to the formality of this grand mansion. Tours by reservation only. Annual events include Christmas open house on the second Sunday of December. The gift shop sells reproductions of Victorian and handmade gifts. No restaurant. Wheelchair access on ground floor. Free parking.

Open Sunday noon–3:30 P.M., Tuesday noon–2:30 P.M., Thursday noon–2:30 P.M. Admission is $1 for adults, 50¢ for senior citizens, children free. Closed during July and August. For more information call (714) 787-7273.

Hi-Desert Nature Museum
57117 Twenty-Nine Palms Hwy, Yucca Valley, CA 92284

GETTING THERE: Take the San Bernardino Fwy (I–10) east to State Hwy 62. Continue on 62 north to where it becomes Twenty-Nine Palms Hwy. Follow to Dumosa Ave. The museum is adjacent to the shopping center.

The museum's brochure is a pleasant introduction to nature study, full of whimsical trivia and a list of museum nature trails. The major exhibits consist of geological samples, gems and fossils, and desert life. The story of Borax and the Famous Twenty-Mule Team is told here along with facts about poisonous and nonpoisonous desert reptiles. A mini-zoo is on display too, along with shells, insects, and collectibles. Films and lectures. Monthly art show. Annual spring wildflower exhibit with displays of specimen and folklore. Educational services include classes, youth group activities, and adult nature study groups. Restaurant and coffee shop, picnic area nearby. Gift shop. Wheelchair access.

Open Wednesday–Sunday 1–5 P.M. Closed Mondays and Tuesdays. Free admission and parking. For more information call (619) 365–9814.

Historical Glass Museum
1157 North Orange, Redlands, CA 92373

GETTING THERE: Take San Bernardino/Redlands Fwy (I–10) east through San Bernardino to Orange Ave. exit. Go north. The museum is located at Orange and Western avenues.

This museum is unique as it is the only West Coast glass museum. Begun by private collectors who wanted to share their love of beautiful glassware, the museum is dedicated to representing every glass manufacturer in the United States as well as numerous craftsmen abroad. Exhibits focus on glass manufacture from 1840 to the present. A magnificent chandelier, believed to be one of the only two made by the Heisley Company still in existence, graces the museum's entrance. Displayed in mirrored cases is a full range of glassware including cut glass from the Brilliant Period, rare colored pressed glass, Steuben glass, patterns from the Cambridge Company, and Sandwich glass. There are glass kerosene lamps and much more.

Iced tea, anyone? Courtesy Historical Glass Museum at Redlands.

Tours by prior arrangement. Slideshows produced by the museum staff are available for rental. Lectures available. Fourteen glass clubs are affiliated with the museum. No restaurant. The gift shop sells glass, china, and limited edition plates. Wheelchair access.

Open to the public on Saturdays only, 11 A.M.–4 P.M. Private tours may be arranged on weekdays one month in advance. Free admission and parking. For information and to arrange tours, write to museum office.

Kimberly Crest House and Gardens
1325 Prospect Dr., Redlands, CA 92373

GETTING THERE: From the San Bernardino Fwy (I–10) take the Orange St. exit south. Orange St. becomes Cajon St. Follow to Highland Ave. Go south on Highland to Alvarado. As Alvarado crosses Highland it becomes Prospect Dr.

Resembling a French chateau, this beautiful 7,000-square-foot home sits on a terraced hill with a view of the San Bernardino Mountains. Built in 1897, its exterior has round towers, steep roof, and window dormers topped with decorative finials. Surrounding Italian gardens include fountains, lily ponds, and pergolas. The 6.5-acre estate also has a variety of eighty-year-old trees and a producing citrus grove.

Gilded Tiffany furniture and lamps, carved rococo revival rosewood furniture, and many opulent details can be found throughout the house, and a musicians' gallery overlooks the main foyer. The permanent collection comprises decorative arts, oriental rugs, and Tiffany pieces.

On the first Sunday of December the museum attracts visitors to its Christmas tree lighting festivities. No gift shop or restaurant. Picnic area in the botanical park adjacent to the house. Free parking. Reservations are required for groups of ten or more.

Open Sunday and Thursday 1–4 P.M. A $2 donation is requested for adults and children. For more information call (714) 792-2111.

The Lincoln Memorial Shrine
125 West Vine St., Redlands, CA 92373

GETTING THERE: Heading east on the San Bernardino Fwy (I-10), take the Orange St.-Downtown exit which ends at Vine St. Turn west on Vine to Eureka. The shrine is located behind the Smiley Library.

This shrine is a tribute to Abraham Lincoln presented to Redlands by Robert and Alma Watchhorn in 1932 honoring Lincoln and memorializing their son who died in World War I. The octagon-shaped shrine was designed by southern California architect Elmer Grey. Excerpts from Lincoln's addresses are inscribed in the limestone walls. Ceiling murals are by New York artist Dean Cornwell, and a well-known marble bust of Lincoln by George Grey Barnard is also here. Collections include documents and letters from Lincoln as well as cabinet members, also coins, stamps, rifles, uniforms, and swords. Also contains an extensive photograph collection. Research library. Films and lectures. Open house on Lincoln's birthday. Wheelchair access and ramps.

Open Tuesday–Saturday 1–5 P.M. Free admission and two-hour street parking. For more information call (714) 798-7632 in the morning or (714) 798-7636 in the afternoon.

Maiki Museum
Morongo Indian Reservation, 110795 Fields Road, Banning, CA 92220

GETTING THERE: Take the San Bernardino Fwy (I-10) east of Banning to the Fields Road exit and follow the sign to the reservation north of the freeway.

The museum is located on the Morongo Indian Reservation and represents the Native American tribes of southern California, with emphasis on the Cahuilla tribe. Artifacts celebrate the origins, cultural history, customs, and music of these California cultures. Collections include basketry, pottery, photography. Annual Memorial Day Fiesta. A 500-volume library in Native American archives and ethnobiological garden is also on the site. Lectures and workshops. Tours available anytime. Wheelchair access.

Open Wednesday–Sunday 10 A.M.–5 P.M. Free admission and parking. For more information call (714) 849-7289.

March Field Museum
March Air Force Base, Riverside, CA 92518

GETTING THERE: Go south on Escondido Fwy (I–215) to March AFB exit, or take Pomona Fwy (60) east to March Air Force Base. Located south of Riverside.

At the oldest air force base in the western U.S. (established as a pilot-training base only fifteen years after the Wright Brothers' first powered flight), this museum depicts military aviation heritage from 1918. Throughout World War II, fighter and bomber crews trained here, and in 1950 it became a Strategic Air Command installation. *The March Field Story* and other Air Force movies are shown in the museum theatre, with prior notice. Tours available for large groups with reservations. Aircraft library. Gift shop, no restaurant. Wheelchair access.

Open weekdays 10 A.M.–4 P.M., Saturday and Sunday noon–4 P.M. Closed on Thanksgiving, Christmas, and New Year's Day. Free admission and parking. For more information call (714) 655-3725.

Mojave River Valley Museum
270 East Virginia Way, Barstow, CA 92311

GETTING THERE: Traveling north of San Bernardino on Barstow Fwy (I–15), go to Barstow Road exit. Continue north on Barstow Road to Virginia Way. The museum is on the corner.

Local history and natural history of the Mojave Desert are featured in this Barstow museum. Examples of gemstones and fossils are displayed in addition to desert animals and the finery of the Victorian period in Barstow. A unique drover car shows how the "drovers," or cattlemen accompanying their cattle, lived in a cabooselike car which sat adjacent to the cattle cars on the train tracks, enabling them to keep an eye on their cattle. Outside the museum is a small, portable jail once used to transport prisoners by wagon or sometimes as a permanent jail cell. The museum is expanding its military and mining displays across the street in a historical park commemorating Barstow's Centennial.

Exhibits here relate the history of the former Casa del Desierto, Barstow's depot-hotel. Serving Santa Fe train passengers en route to the West Coast, this active depot and the famous Harvey House Hotel is a fascinating part of railroad and Barstow history. Films and lectures. Call for information on tours. Visit "May Open House" and barbecue. Library open by appointment. Educational services include monthly programs and field trips, youth group activities. Gift shop. No restaurant. Wheelchair access.

Open weekdays 8 A.M.–5 P.M. and Saturdays and Sundays 11 A.M.–4 P.M. Free admission and parking. For more information call (619) 253-2954.

Ontario Museum of History and Art
225 South Euclid Ave., Ontario, CA 91761

GETTING THERE: From San Bernardino Fwy (I–10) exit onto Euclid Ave. and continue south one block past Holt Blvd. to Transit St.

Built in 1903 as a country club and used later as the Ontario City Hall, this handsome, mission-style building is now the home of an art and historical museum. The art wing provides exhibition galleries for the museum's fine arts collection and for exhibitions and art competitions largely pertaining to California artists from the 1930s to the present. The permanent collection includes works by Rex Brandt, Millard Sheets, Phil Dike, Henry Lee McFee, and Jean Ames. Housed in the history wing since 1983 are permanent historical exhibits of Ontario's local history and culture. Past temporary shows have been on weaving, trade beads, and the history of the General Electric Hotpoint iron. Special programs include films, lectures, workshops, and video presentations. Art classes offered, including Chinese brush painting. The adjacent former city council room is being restored for use as an educational center. Annual events include the permanent collection show in July and August, and the art competition in January and February. Gift shop. Adjacent park has picnic tables. Wheelchair access and parking.

Open Thursday–Sunday 1–5 P.M. Free admission and parking. For more information call (714) 983-3198.

Palm Springs Desert Museum

101 Museum Dr., Palm Springs, CA 92263

GETTING THERE: The museum is located ten miles south of the San Bernardino Fwy (I–10) via Palm Canyon Dr. From Palm Canyon, turn west on Tahquitz-McCallum Way and north on Museum Dr.

The combination of collections in this museum is unusual in that it combines fine arts, natural science, and performing arts. In the handsome, 75,000-square-foot split-level cantilevered building visitors will see contemporary and western American art and many private collections and works of local artists and artisans. The natural science area exhibits the plants, geology, and animals of the Palm Springs area, and depicts desert life by day and night in long, colorful dioramas. In addition to these galleries are the two fine sunken sculpture gardens and a sculpture courtyard.

The museum houses a 3,500-volume library of art and natural science books, and a large auditorium for special events. Collections include western American and contemporary art, natural history, natural science, sculpture, graphics, geology, ethnology, and archaeology. Gallery talks, concerts, and dance recitals are regularly scheduled. Nature trail on museum grounds. Museum tours are conducted Tuesday–Saturday at 2 P.M. Also arranged by appointment. Educational services include films, lectures, workshops, and community outreach for elementary through high school grade levels.

The gift shop sells Indian silver and jewelry, Kachina dolls, baskets, rugs, contemporary gifts and books, children's arts and craft sets. No restaurant. Wheelchair access and parking. Parking is free.

Open Tuesday–Sunday 10 A.M.–5 P.M. Closed Mondays. Admission is $3 for adults, $1.50 for children. For more information call (619) 325-7186 or (619) 325-0189.

Planes of Fame Air Museum

Chino Airport, 7000 Merrill Ave., Chino, CA 91710

GETTING THERE: Take the San Bernardino Fwy (I-10) or the Pomona Fwy (60) east to Euclid Ave. exit. Go south on Euclid (83) to the Chino Airport. From Orange County, take Riverside Fwy (91) east to the Corona Fwy (71). Drive north to Euclid (83). Follow to airport entrance.

Anyone who likes airplanes or watching World War II movies will enjoy this outdoor museum at the Chino Airport. Visitors wander around craft and climb inside pilots' seats and gunners' bubbles, or engage in one of the most interesting activities on site, talking with former crew members of World War II aircraft. The veterans volunteer their time on weekends to be here, and their fascinating scrapbooks are on display. In one hangar is housed a unique collection of flyable aircraft, including a Messerschmitt ME262 Schwalbe, a P26A Peashooter, a Spirit of Bataan Seversky Pursuit, a Japanese Cherry Blossom, and a motorless, pilot-guided suicide craft. The only remaining flyable Japanese Zero in the world is also here.

The Air Museum is dedicated to restoring as many "birds" as possible, and in another hangar the restoration is in progress. Young and not-so-young airplane enthusiasts meticulously work on both exterior shells and small aircraft parts. Films and lectures available. Annual airshow in May. Tours. Call for reservations. Special programs at the May Air Show. The gift shop sells model kits, video cassettes of airshows, souvenirs. No restaurant. Wheelchair access.

Open daily 9 A.M.–5 P.M. Closed on Christmas. Admission is $3.95 for adults, $1.95 for children. Free parking. For more information call (714) 597-3722.

Riverside Art Museum

3425 7th St., Riverside, CA 92501

GETTING THERE: Take Riverside Fwy (91) to the 7th St. exit, go west, and proceed to 3425 7th St.

Although housed in the distinctive 1928 YMCA building designed by Julia Morgan (assistant architect for Hearst Castle), the museum houses a respectable collection of modern and contemporary California arts and crafts with emphasis on watercolorists

One of the restored "birds" at Planes of Fame Air Museum. Photo by Sara LeBien.

including Rex Brent and Joan Irvine Brandt. All shows are juried and two major shows are presented each year.

The museum offers a strong art program and activity workshops for children. One in particular is the Fun-in-the-Sun weekend art festival. Workshops include crafts, ceramics, batik, woodworking, and print-making. Tours available. Call for reservation. Films and lectures, six studios, art rental program. Annual events include Buy-Art-for-Christmas event, decorator show, and a juried offering of art for purchase corresponding with weekend festivals. Restaurant. The gift shop sells a wide assortment of original art work—jewelry, textiles, pottery, glass, sculpture, painting, prints, and art books.

Open Monday 10 A.M.–3 P.M., Tuesday–Friday 10 A.M.–5 P.M., Saturday 10 A.M.–4 P.M. Closed Sundays. Admission is free. For information call (714) 684-7111.

Riverside Municipal Museum
3720 Orange St., Riverside, CA 92501

GETTING THERE: Take Riverside Fwy (91) to 7th St. exit. Proceed west to Orange, and turn left. The museum is across the street from the public library.

Originally founded through the acquisition of a fine Indian basket collection, for which the museum received international recognition, the Riverside Municipal Museum features local history, anthropology, and natural history. Exhibits depict Riverside's historical heritage from 1774 to the present, including important exhibits on the citrus industry. Western Native American culture, as portrayed by artifacts recovered from excavations at Riverside's Chinatown, are also on display. The local geology displays include rocks and fossils. Heritage House, an elaborate Victorian mansion and historical museum, belongs to the Riverside Museum. Permanent collections include Native American artifacts, baskets, paleontology, geology, and anthropology exhibits. Educational services include lecture series, classes, field trips, outreach programs, and publications. Tours by reservation only. Also films and lectures. Gift shop. No restaurant. Wheelchair access, parking and elevator.

Open Tuesday–Friday 9 A.M.–5 P.M. and on weekends 1–5 P.M. Closed Mondays. Free admission and parking. For more information call (714) 787-7273.

Roy Rogers and Dale Evans Museum
15650 Seneca Road, Victorville, CA 92392

GETTING THERE: Take Barstow Fwy (I-15) to the Palmdale Road exit. The museum is visible from the highway at Seneca and Civic Dr. west of the freeway. Take Palmdale Road west to Amargosa, turn north, then east on Civic Dr.

In a museum modeled after an army fort, a lifetime of personal and career memorabilia are on display for the many fans of Roy Rogers and Dale Evans. Considered to be the best personal museum in the United States it has three main exhibition halls to house major collections of family heirlooms, antiques and dolls, Roy Rogers' collection of mounted trophies, and part of an extensive gun collection. Authentically detailed scale models of western vehicles provide a history of trans-Mississippi transportation. No restaurant. Gift shop.

Open daily 9 A.M.–5 P.M. Closed on Thanksgiving and Christmas. Admission is $3 for adults, $2 for juniors, $1 for children, $2 for senior citizens 65 and over. For more information call (619) 243-4547.

San Bernardino County Museum
2024 Orange Tree Lane, Redlands, CA 92373

GETTING THERE: Take the San Bernardino Fwy (I-10) east to the California St. exit. Go north to Orange Tree Lane, turn right. Museum is located on the western edge of Redlands.

Widely known to be an exciting place for children to visit. The signs say "Please Touch" and "Please Handle," and visitors are encouraged to handle the small animals and reptiles. Bird songs fill the exhibition hall housing bird and egg displays (over 100,000 eggs in permanent collection!) including the elephant bird egg which can hold over two gallons of liquid. Dioramas feature mammals of North America, a Hall of History with an authentic prairie schooner on exhibit, and San Bernardino in 1851, when it was still

Exhibit of the nearly extinct California condor. Courtesy San Bernardino County Museum.

a military fort. Annual events include Waterfowl West, a prestigious duck stamp show competition. The gift shop sells contemporary jewelry set with semiprecious stones, geodes and crystals, fool's gold, and large selection of books on Native Americans, minerals, mining, birds, and dinosaurs. Picnic area. Wheelchair access and parking.

Open Tuesday–Saturday 9 A.M.–5 P.M. and Sunday 1 P.M.–5 P.M. The small animal and reptile exhibits are open Friday, Saturday, and Sunday 1–4 P.M. Free admission and parking. For more information call (714) 792-1334 and (714) 825-4825.

Sherman Indian Museum
9010 Magnolia Ave., Riverside, CA 92503

GETTING THERE: Coming from Los Angeles take Riverside Fwy (91) to the Van Buren exit, go west, then turn right on Andrews St. Follow to Jackson St., at which point you will see the school.

The Sherman Institute, originally a federal boarding school for Native American youths, was established in 1902 and is now one of the few institutions of its kind still in operation. Students from Hopi, Apache, and several northern and southern California coastline tribes attend classes here. Located in the original administration building, this museum houses Native American artifacts donated through the years by former students, including a Hopi kilt, a Sioux bandolier (a beaded ceremonial costume), Kachina dolls, beadwork, pottery, and pre-Columbian artifacts. Dioramas depict diversity of Indian cultures. Lectures, tours by reservation only. Library open to the public. Schools may arrange for museum staff to visit with presentation. Free parking. No restaurant or shop. Wheelchair access and special parking.

Open weekdays 1–3 P.M. Closed on weekends and all school holidays. Admission by donation. For more information call (714) 359-9434.

Chapter Eight

San Gabriel Valley— Pasadena to Claremont

Adobe de Palomares
491 East Arrow Highway, Pomona, CA 91767

GETTING THERE: Located one mile north of the San Bernardino Fwy (I-10). Exit at Towne Ave. and go north to Arrow Highway. Go west just beyond Orange Grove, between Towne and Garey.

Located on acreage that was formerly called Rancho San Jose, this traditional adobe belonged to two early Spanish settlers. Furnished in the 1800s period, the adobe was the home of the Palomares family, and their adjoining blacksmith shop is furnished with many of the original tools. Family documents and diaries were researched to reconstruct the gardens. Once used for both cooking and medicinal purposes, the herb garden has been re-established, and the original wisteria, grapevines, and roses still flourish. Two weeks' notice required for tours. Annual events include Adobe Days in March, commemorating the Feast of St. Joseph, patron saint of the rancho, which is highlighted with folk dancing, Spanish food, music, and craft demonstrations. The gift shop offers postcards, stationery, and history books. Picnic area. Limited wheelchair access.

Open Sunday–Tuesday 2–5 P.M. Free admission and parking. For more information call (714) 620–2300.

The Raymond M. Alf Museum

1175 West Base Line Road, Claremont, CA 91711

GETTING THERE: Take the Towne Ave. exit off the San Bernardino Fwy (I-10), north to Base Line Road, left to the entrance between Garey and Towne Ave. It is on the campus of the Webb School.

When school teacher Raymond M. Alf led fossil-collecting trips for Webb School in 1938, his students' collections grew through the years and later found a permanent home. The chakrah-style museum building is filled with displays on evolution. A tour entitled "From Stars to Early Civilization" in the Hall of Life traces the history of earth life from 3.5 billion years ago through Egyptian and American Indian civilizations. The focus of this collection is fossil insects and plants as well as fossil mammals and Ban Chiang pottery.

The Hall of Fossil Footprints contains the largest and most diverse display of these artifacts in the United States, including footprints of spiders, scorpions, reptiles, dinosaurs, birds, elephants, and amphibians. Two unique displays are the prints of a giant 15 million-year-old bear dog, the oldest mammal footprint in North America, and the installation on pre-Cambrian cellular evolution which is unsurpassed among North American museums. Group tours by appointment.

The museum is used as a learning center for students, parents, educators, and scientists, and its programs invite active participation in personal exploration and discovery. Members of the museum's Peccary Society have opportunities to travel and participate in paleontological explorations, including family fossil-collecting trips, foreign tours, paleontology classes, and a four-week summer trip through the Southwest. High school students from all over the world are invited to apply for this summer program. The museum has a bookstore and gift shop and local parks nearby permit picnics. Free parking. Wheelchair access and special parking.

The museum is open from September to May, Tuesday–Friday 9 A.M. –noon and 1–4 P.M. Also open one Saturday each month. Closed on school holidays and during summer months. Donations welcome. For more information call (714) 626-3587, ext. 216.

George Anderson House
215 East Lime Ave., Monrovia, CA 91016

GETTING THERE: Go north from the Foothill Fwy (I-210) on Myrtle Ave. to Lime Ave. Go right on Lime 1½ blocks. The house is next to the police station.

When the city of Monrovia was founded in 1886, John Anderson who erected its first building, the Monrovia Hotel, built this home for his family. Completely refurbished, Monrovia's Heritage Home displays antique furniture, including a beautiful five-piece bird's-eye maple bedroom suite, as well as an 1850 sewing machine, a child's four-poster canopy bed, and an old pump organ which visitors may play. Collections include local historical memorabilia and furnishings of the 1880–1910 period. Museum library. Slide presentations and lectures about other historic sites. Tours available for elementary and high school classes and special groups. Christmas holiday decor and antique pump organ entertainment scheduled annually. No eating facilities or wheelchair access.

Open the third Sunday of each month, 1–4 P.M. Free admission and parking. For more information and to reserve tours write to museum office.

El Molino Viejo Museum—The Old Mill
1120 Old Mill Road, San Marino, CA 91108

GETTING THERE: Take the Foothill Fwy (I-210) to the Lake Avenue exit. Go south. Lake becomes Oak Knoll Ave. At the first stop sign past the Huntington Hotel, turn left onto Old Mill Road.

Tucked away in a beautiful San Marino residential area, El Molino Viejo looks more like a charming, secluded weekend retreat than a water-powered grist mill, the first in southern California. It was built by Indian laborers from the San Gabriel Mission in about 1816. Visitors can see the grinding room water wheel and wheel chamber below, and exhibitions on California history, the mill-works, prospecting, and mining methods. With five and one-half-foot thick walls, original peg floors, and massive ceiling beams, the rooms display a few pieces of old Spanish furniture.

Now owned by the City of San Marino, the mill is the southern California headquarters of the California Historical Society, which provides interesting changing exhibitions here at the mill. The

145

The George Anderson House reflects the 1880–1910 period. Photo by Sara LeBien.

Society's history center on Wilshire Boulevard is a repository for 15,000 photographs pertaining to California history. Self-guided tours. No wheelchair access or eating facilities.

Open Tuesday–Sunday 1–4 P.M. Closed Mondays and holidays. Free admission and parking. For more information and tour arrangements call (818) 449-5450.

El Monte Museum of History
3150 Tyler Ave., El Monte, CA 91731

GETTING THERE: Take the San Bernardino Fwy (I–10) east to the Santa Anita exit. Go east five blocks to Tyler. Museum is one block south of the freeway.

In 1851 a wagon train of pioneers settled on this fertile acreage with both water and woods, the area was called *monte,* meaning "wooded spot," and the captain of the expedition named the village Lexington, after his Kentucky home. The museum building is a former library and the collections are displayed in room settings representing a house and shops of the period between 1850 and the 1890s. In addition to the Victorian period furnishings, costumes and residential stained glass, are a general store, schoolhouse, two-bedroom house, hat shop, and dress shop. A Spanish Colonial exhibit is in the Frontier Room; Child's World is a display of toys, furniture, and clothing that belonged to children in the 1800s. There are also a train depot and fire department as well as an outside courtyard exhibiting wagons of that era. Tours by appointment. Annual events include Christmas reception, Historical Society annual dinner, and club meetings. Gift shop. No eating facilities. Wheelchair access and special parking.

Open Tuesday–Saturday 10 A.M.–4 P.M. Free admission but donations are appreciated. For more information and to reserve tours call (818) 444-3813.

The Gamble House
4 Westmoreland Place, Pasadena, CA 91103

GETTING THERE: Take Ventura Fwy (134) to Orange Grove Blvd. exit. Go north. Westmoreland Place is a private street entered through driveways intersecting the 300 block of North Orange Grove Blvd between Arroyo Terrace and Rosemont.

Built by noted Pasadena architects Henry and Charles Greene, this house is considered to be one of the finest examples of the American craftsman movement. It is a masterpiece of architecture and home design. The uniqueness of the house evolved from the brothers' fascination with Japanese joinery and their respect for natural materials. Their many innovations included hand-shaped beams and projecting rafters permitting open sleeping porches, creatively handcrafted wood, wrought-iron furnishings, and Tiffany glass.

Educational services include a junior docent program for gifted eighth graders that trains students to conduct tours for young school groups. Guided tours are provided to the public during regular hours. Groups of ten or more require a reservation arranged at least one month in advance. The gift shop offers slides, stationery, craft and architecture books, including books on Japanese joinery. Limited street parking. No restaurants or wheelchair facilities.

Open Tuesday and Thursday 10 A.M.–3 P.M., Sunday noon–3 P.M., except major holidays. Admission is $4 for adults, $3 for senior citizens over 65, $2 for college students. High school students and younger are free. For more information call (213) 681-6427.

The Huntington Library Art Collections and Botanical Gardens
1151 Oxford Road, San Marino, CA 91108

GETTING THERE: From Foothill Fwy (I–210) west take the Allen exit south to the Huntington gate. From the San Bernardino Fwy (I–10), take the San Gabriel Blvd. exit north; turn left on California Blvd. and left again on Allen; proceed south to the Huntington gate.

The former residence of Henry E. Huntington, railroad magnate and art collector, this beautiful home is divided into three main exhibition areas. The Gallery contains the most comprehensive collection of British eighteenth- and nineteenth-century art outside of London. Its main room displays Gainsborough's famous *Blue Boy*, Lawrence's *Pinkie*, Reynold's *Mrs. Siddons As the Tragic Muse*, and Constable's *View on the Stour*. Throughout the house are drawings, furniture, silver, miniatures, sculpture, and ceramics.

*The Huntington Library Art Collection and Botanical Gardens is the world's larg-
est plant collection/art museum. Photo by Sara LeBien.*

The Library's four galleries house renaissance paintings and eighteenth-century French sculpture, tapestries, porcelain, and furniture, also two hundred notable rare book treasures, including early editions of Shakespeare's plays, an illustrated manuscript of Chaucer's *Canterbury Tales*, Audubon's *Birds of America*, Benjamin Franklin's autobiography, and a Gutenberg Bible.

The Virginia Steele Scott Gallery exhibits American art from the 1740s to the 1930s. The permanent collections contain portraits by Peter Vanderlyn, Robert Feke, John Singleton Copley, Walt Kuhn, and John Stewart Curry; figurative paintings by Benjamin West and Mary Cassatt; western landscapes by Thomas Moran; and many twentieth-century works.

Spanning 207 acres, the continually blooming botanical gardens contain twelve horticultural and botanical displays. The north vista has Italian statuary and world-renowned camellia collection representing one thousand varieties which bloom from autumn through April. The Shakespeare garden displays colorful seasonal plants and flowers, and the rose garden has more than 1,200 varieties arranged in historical sequence. The jungle garden contains tropical plants and a waterfall, and the desert garden comprises the largest outdoor collection of desert plants in the world. The Japanese garden is a five-acre canyon below a large bronze temple bell placed at the entrance, and contains a furnished Japanese house, a Zen garden, and a bonsai court. Its mellow gong can be heard repeatedly as visitors succumb to the temptation of striking it before descending the steps to the garden.

Special children's programs and tours. A ten-minute introductory film is presented at frequent intervals, and docent-led tours of the gardens are available at 1 P.M. on posted schedule. A staff member in the library hall will provide information. Self-guided tour leaflets of the galleries and gardens are for sale. The Southern California Research Center of the Archives of American Art is in the Scott Gallery.

The gift shop sells a wide assortment of books, plant cuttings, posters, prints, publications, slides, and cards. The Garden Restaurant offers both cafeteria and tea room service 1–4 P.M. daily. There is a car drop-off area near the entrance, elevators in the galleries, and wheelchair access on garden paths.

Open Tuesday–Sunday 1–4:30 P.M. Advanced reservations required on Sundays. Closed on major holidays. Suggested donation of $2 per adult. A $2 fee is charged at the parking entrance and includes parking and entrance to the buildings. For a recorded message call (818) 405–2280 or for more information call (818) 405–2100.

Los Angeles County Arboretum
301 North Baldwin Ave., Arcadia, CA 90031

GETTING THERE: Take the San Bernardino Fwy (I–10) to the Baldwin Ave. exit. Go north on Baldwin to the entrance on the west side of the street. From the Foothill Fwy (I–210), take the Baldwin exit and go south to Arboretum entrance.

This arboretum is well known for its beautiful botanical gardens and as a teaching institution, but it is also a significant historic site. The land was once a Gabrieliño Indian village, hence the name "San Gabriel Valley." As part of the later mission holdings it became Rancho Santa Anita. The original rancho adobe has been reconstructed and refurnished complete with outdoor stove and oven. During the 1800s large California ranchos were gradually acquired by businessmen. In 1875 "Lucky Baldwin," fulfilling his investment ambitions in southern California, bought Rancho Santa Anita and constructed a lavish Queen Anne-style cottage on the grounds. Through prudent management the ranch reached its full potential in the 1800s when nearly 8,000 acres were planted with fields, orchards, vineyards, and citrus groves. The ranch was later a film site for *On the Road to Singapore* with Bob Hope and Bing Crosby, *Tarzan and the Hunters* with Johnny Weissmuller, and *African Queen* with Humphrey Bogart and Katharine Hepburn. The same spring-fed lagoon which had attracted the Indians to this land is where Humphrey Bogart pulled the *African Queen* through the jungle.

There are also Indian wickiups, or nomadic huts, the Hugo Reid Adobe and courtyard, a Queen Anne cottage with Victorian furnishings, coach barn with buggies, tack room, and blacksmith shop. Other interesting features are a Santa Anita Depot with refurnished railroad equipment and household furnishings, bromeliad greenhouse, begonia greenhouse, a garden for all seasons, shade garden, tropical greenhouse with Australian section, and South African section. Tour book available. The arboretum also has programs on plant production and conservation. Educational services include guided field trips on local history and garden programs, and Plants of Man can be arranged in advance for school tours. The Peacock Pavilion has a coffee shop and a gift shop offering a wide assortment of plants, books, handcrafted items and arranged dried flowers, posters, film, and postcards. Special parking, wheelchair access on all paved walkways.

Open daily 9 A.M.–4:30 P.M. Closed on Christmas. Admission is $3 for adults, $1.50 for children 5–17 and senior citizens over 62. For more information call (818) 446-8251.

Mission San Gabriel
537 West Mission Dr., San Gabriel, CA 91776

GETTING THERE: From the San Bernardino Fwy (I–10) take the New Ave. exit north to Mission Dr., turn right.

Built in 1771, this was the fourth mission to be established along the El Camino Real, the "King's Highway," when California was part of the Spanish empire. With 9,000 members, it is still active. Constructed in 1812, the museum is nearly 300 feet long and is comprised of several rooms. Cisterns for boiling soap and tanks for tanning hides portray early mission life and an old aqueduct and several outdoor fireplaces for cooking are also on view. In one section of the courtyard is a cemetery centered with a prominent, large wooden crucifix as a memorial to 6,000 Indians buried within the mission grounds.

Museum artifacts include embroidered and hand-painted vestments used by the early mission padres, Indian baskets, Bibles dating as early as 1548, wine-making equipment, and an assortment of tools. One room displays old priceless books and another houses oil paintings of the Fourteen Stations of the Cross, probably the oldest Indian-made religious art on canvas in California. Self-guided tours. Excellent brochure and map. Tours for school groups are available by reservation only. The gift shop has an assortment of religious items, children's books, and souvenirs. No restaurant or picnic area. Wheelchair access. Free parking.

Although the museum is temporarily closed for earthquake repairs, both the gardens and the church are open daily 9:30 A.M.–4:15 P.M. Closed on Easter, Thanksgiving, and Christmas. On Sundays two masses are offered in English, one in Spanish, and one in Vietnamese. Museum admission is $1 for adults, 50¢ for children ages 5–12, age 4 and under are free. For more information call (818) 282-5191.

Mission San Gabriel still calls members to mass. Photo by Sara LeBien.

Pacific Asia Museum
46 North Los Robles Ave., Pasadena, CA 91101

GETTING THERE: Take the Pasadena Fwy (110) to the Colorado Blvd. exit, go east to Los Robles, north ½ block. From Foothill Fwy (I–210) exit south on Los Robles Ave.

Resembling a Chinese imperial palace and courtyard, the museum opened in 1926, after its authenticity had been assured by having decorative roof tiles, stone, marble carvings, and bronze work made in China and then assembled by Pasadena craftsmen. The completed Chinese garden simulates a traditional Chinese landscape painting. Its rocks, water, zigzag bridge, Koi fish, and plantings provide a tranquil haven in downtown Pasadena.

Unique as the only institution in southern California specializing in the arts of Asia and the Pacific Basin, this museum has several exquisite collections representing the art of China, Japan, the Philippines, India, Korea, and Thailand. It also hosts cultures of the Pacific Basin, with eleven different volunteer groups who conduct programs highlighting these diverse cultural traditions. Rotating exhibits on China Trade, Chinese Jade, and "The Image from Within" appear in the Foyer Gallery. The primary collections here are Japanese paintings of the Edo and early Meiji periods, Paul Jacoulet prints, ceramics and religious sculpture from China, Tibet, Nepal, Cambodia, and Japan. Also Southeast Asian ceramics of the fourteenth and fifteenth centuries and miniatures from China, Japan, and Nepal.

Special programs for the public include guided tours, lectures, live demonstrations, films, performances, and travel programs. The museum also hosts an annual Festival of the Autumn Moon and an annual Star Festival. The museum has a formally organized education program. School tours are encouraged and a speaker's service is available. Research library.

For tour reservations, call (818) 449-2742. Public tours are held each Saturday at 2 P.M. The gift shop offers books, posters, paper gifts, and oriental decorative arts. A variety of small shops are also located on the first and second floors. No restaurant, but neighborhood eating establishments are within walking distance. No

Exquisite carved pendant from the Sung Dynasty (960–1280 A.D.), on view at the Pacific Asia Museum. Photo by Don Farber.

The peaceful serenity of a Chinese palace courtyard found in downtown Pasadena. Courtesy Pacific Asia Museum. Photo by Don Farber.

wheelchair facilities except access on street level into main exhibition area.

Open Wednesday–Sunday noon–5 P.M. Admission is $2 for adults, $1.50 for senior citizens, and students, children under 12 free if accompanied by an adult. Free admission on third Saturday of each month. For more information call (818) 449-2742.

Pasadena Historical Society Museum—Fenyes House
470 West Walnut St., Pasadena, CA 91103

GETTING THERE: From the Ventura Fwy (134), take North Orange Grove Blvd. to West Walnut St. The mansion is directly across the freeway from the Norton Simon Art Museum.

Once a center for social and cultural functions, this is one of the few early grand homes remaining in Pasadena. Designed in 1905 to resemble an Italian villa, the house is furnished with exquisite pieces from all over the world. One unusual piece is a tenth-century Spanish chest with secret compartments possibly for hiding valuables during the Spanish Inquisition. Tapestries, family portraits, carved chests, and a Tiffany lamp are just a few of the magnificent furnishings. There are also early Pasadena memorabilia, maps, photos, manuscripts. In addition to the family living areas is a solarium, used by the family as a greenhouse, and a studio which was not only used for painting, but for receptions, plays, and teas. Once designated as the Finnish Consulate in southern California, the house now has a Finnish folk art exhibition, and a sauna house contains artifacts representing eighteenth-century rural life in Finland. Archives are maintained by Finlandia Foundation.

Historic photo reproductions are available. Speakers and slide presentations for schools and groups. Luncheon is served occasionally on Wednesdays from June to October. Reservations required. Historic hikes are conducted by volunteers through the Arroyo Seco, Eaton Canyon, Mt. Lowe, and other sites in the San Gabriel Mountains. Special events such as concerts, art exhibits, and craft seminars are held, as well as docent-led tours of local historic sites. The Edwardian Christmas program is an annual event at the museum.

Guided one-hour tours begin every 15 minutes. Last tour begins at 3 P.M. The gift shop offers an assortment of publications on Pasadena, handmade gifts, antiques, greeting cards, and cookbooks. No wheelchair or eating facilities.

Open Tuesday, Thursday and the first and last Sunday of the month, 1–4 P.M. Admission is $3 for adults, $2 for students with ID and senior citizens. For more information call (818) 577–1660.

Norton Simon Museum
411 West Colorado Blvd., Pasadena, CA 91105

GETTING THERE: The museum is located right at the junction of Foothill (I–210) and Ventura (134) freeways. At the corner of Orange Grove and Colorado boulevards, the striking black-and-white building is visible from the freeway.

This museum is seen each year by millions who watch the Rose Bowl Parade on television. Unlike typical linear galleries, the museum interior has rounded edges and curves instead of corners, giving a peaceful environment for works of art and for the viewer.

The Norton Simon art collection is one of the finest in the country. Its holdings include European paintings from the early renaissance to mid-twentieth century, one of the best collections of stone and bronze sculpture from India and Southeast Asia in the world, and an extensive collection of Picasso graphics. Enormous and exquisite tapestries grace the museum walls. The art collection is a feast to behold, including works by Chardin, Corot, Manet, Cezanne, Courbet, Seurat, Monet, Degas, Raphael, Botticelli, Rubens, Matisse, van Gogh, Klee, Tiepolo, and Fragonard. The museum also has a distinguished sculpture collection with works by Renoir, Degas and twentieth-century sculptors Rodin, Maillol, Hepworth, Brancusi, Lipchitz, and Moore. The sculptures are located throughout the museum and in the garden outside.

Group tours available (for twenty-five or more). Call (818) 449–6840 or (213) 681–2484. Adjoining sculpture garden and reflecting pool. The museum has an excellent bookstore. No eating facilities. Free parking. Wheelchair access, ramps and special parking.

Francisco Zurbarn's oil painting, Still Life: Lemons, Oranges and a Rose, *is found at the Norton Simon Museum. Courtesy of Norton Simon Foundation.*

Open Thursday–Sunday noon–6 P.M. Admission is $2 for adults, 75¢ for students and senior citizens 62 and over. Children under 12 and members are free. For more information call (818) 449-6840.

Chapter Nine

Hollywood and Griffith Park

Forest Lawn Memorial-Parks (Hollywood Hills)
6300 Forest Lawn Dr., Los Angeles, CA 90068

GETTING THERE: Take the Ventura Fwy (134) to the Forest Lawn exit. Go west on Forest Lawn Dr. to the entrance. The park is adjacent to the northern boundary of Griffith Park.

While Forest Lawn Memorial Park in Glendale features works of famous artists and unusual artistic accomplishments, the Forest Lawn Memorial Park in Hollywood Hills is a tribute to American history through film, art, and museum-style exhibits. On these grounds visitors will find a number of historical and legendary recreations. One is a reproduction of the "Church of the Hills," where Henry Wadsworth Longfellow worshipped as a boy. Inside is the Longfellow Historical Room, where personal mementos, handwritten documents, and family portraits are on display.

Another site is the Old North Church immortalized in Longfellow's poem, "Paul Revere's Ride." Recreated with a historical room, it houses documents and artifacts including Paul Revere's personal account of his ride, maps drawn by Captain John Smith, and engravings by Paul Revere.

Continuing along the main road, at the top of the hill visitors will come upon *The Birth of Liberty*, an outdoor mosaic on the exterior wall of the Hall of Liberty. Comprised of 10 million pieces of Venetian glass, it is the largest historical mosaic in the U.S. The mosaic reproduces twenty-five famous American paintings and statues, depicting American history from 1619 to 1787. In the Hall of Liberty is a museum exhibiting reproductions and artifacts of the Revolutionary War and the Declaration of Independence.

161

The Birth of Liberty *is the largest historical mosaic in the United States. Courtesy of Forest Lawn Memorial-Parks, Hollywood Hills.*

Reproductions of uniforms, historical papers, the Crown Jewels of England, the Liberty Bell, and several original works of art are on display. A film entitled *Many Voices of Freedom*, a portrait of the Revolutionary period, is shown here. It is recommended that visitors see this before viewing the mosaic outside.

Yet another beautiful mosaic, found at Lincoln Terrace, depicts the life of Lincoln. It is near a bronze statue of Lincoln, considered to be the finest portrait statue in the U.S.

In the Court of Liberty there are two original statues, a ten-foot bronze of Thomas Jefferson and a sixty-foot monument to George Washington. Washington's four distinguished generals, Lafayette, Knox, Greene, and Benjamin Lincoln, are also honored here.

Appealing to the large Hispanic population in southern California, Forest Lawn Hollywood Hills has added a Museum of Mexican History. In a gallery inside the Hall of Liberty are exhibitions which explore the early civilizations of Mexico. Contributions made by the Olmecs, Zapotecs, Mixtecs, Maya, Totonacs, Toltecs, Aztecs, and the people of Teotihuacán are highlighted. Installations with both English and Spanish captions display photographs, maps, beautiful reproductions of early imaginative ceramics, and colorful woven costumes. Other exhibits focus on these civilizations' contributions to astronomy, mathematics, art, and architecture.

Outside in the Plaza of Mexican Heritage is a small garden displaying seventeen reproductions of carved artifacts from Mexico. Intricate, hand-sculpted mosaics, monuments, heads, *steles* (carved stones), and a calendar stone are surrounded by desert plants native to the early cultures of Mexico. Brochures provide a self-guided tour.

Concerts are held in the Hall of Liberty. Call Community Affairs Office for this and other programs at (213) 254–3131 or (818) 241–4151. The West Coast Sacred Torch Ceremony is held on Veterans Day on November 11. No restaurants. Picnics are prohibited. Wheelchair access into Hall of Liberty and auditorium through a back door.

The Hall of Liberty is open weekdays 10 A.M.–1:30 P.M. and from 10 A.M.–4 P.M. on Saturday and Sunday. Admission and parking are free.

163

Frank Lloyd Wright's Hollyhock House
4800 Hollywood Blvd., Los Angeles, CA 90027

GETTING THERE: Take the Hollywood Fwy (U.S. 101) to the Hollywood Blvd. exit. Go east into Barnsdall Park and drive to the top of the hill.

An important landmark for anyone interested in the history of architecture, Frank Lloyd Wright's design philosophy of "organic architecture" (half-house, half-garden) is evident in this house designed by him in 1920 for oil millionairess Aline Barnsdall. Significant architectural features are Wright's effective use of angles, space, and varying floor levels. Some of his innovations evident here are built-in furniture, covered overhead lighting, radiant heat, concrete used as a decorative building material, and wall-hung commodes. A stylized hollyhock design rendered in wood, concrete, and glass is visible throughout both the interior and exterior of the house.

Aline Barnsdall envisioned a hilltop colony for the arts and the artists including housing, shops, children's play school and zoo, theaters, and crafts center. The main house, a second house, drama theater, and movie theater are now part of Barnsdall Park, a Los Angeles municipal art center. The second house serves as a crafts center, and the Municipal Art Gallery, its exterior compatible with the houses, presents ongoing arts festivals and exhibitions.

The main house is open for tours and provides insights into the unique personality, life, and vision of Frank Lloyd Wright. No gift shop or restaurant on the grounds but many can be found along Hollywood Boulevard. Hot-dog stands in the park during special events. Ample picnic area. Free curbside parking along the road winding through the park. Limited wheelchair access in the main house.

Admission is $1.50 for adults, $1 for seniors 62 and older. Free for students under 18 touring with a class and an adult and for children 12 and younger when accompanied by an adult. Purchase tickets in the Municipal Art Gallery. Public tours are offered on Tuesday, Wednesday, and Thursday at 10 and 11 A.M., noon, and 1 P.M.; Saturday and the first, second, and third Sundays, at noon, 1, 2 and 3 P.M. Reservations for tours in foreign languages may be made one month in advance by calling (213) 485-4580 Monday–Thursday 8:30 A.M.–4:30 P.M. For more information call (213) 662-7272.

Gene Autry Western Heritage Museum
Griffith Park, Los Angeles, CA 90027

GETTING THERE: From the Ventura Fwy (134) or the Golden State Fwy (I-5) take the Zoo Drive exit to the museum. It can be seen from the freeway directly across from the Griffith Park Zoo parking lot.

Opening in Fall 1988, this museum will house one of the most comprehensive collections of western American history in the world, presenting a historical survey spanning the period from the Spanish explorers to the present day. Located on thirteen rolling acres, the building's trilevel architecture is a contemporary adaptation of the Southwest mission design.

Fascinating objects include western art, firearms, furnishings, clothing, toys, and games used by both the famous and the ordinary in western history. They include art works by Frederic Remington and Charles Russell as well as hundreds of beautiful saddles and personal memorabilia of cowboy film stars including Tom Mix, Gene Autry, and John Wayne.

Seven permanent galleries celebrate the spirit of western America with theme displays entitled "Discovery," "Opportunity," "Conquest," "Community," "Romance," "Imagination," and "The Cowboy." Trappers, Indians, traders, merchants, craftsmen, and pioneer families will be documented in photographic displays and memorabilia. Later development of the telegraph, stage line, and railroad will also be featured. The Spirit of Romance display is comprised of the literary and artistic interpretations of this heritage which fostered the exciting romance of the West. Two galleries are devoted to rotating exhibitions and shows.

The museum also has a research library and archives center, an education facility, and a 238-seat theater for viewing western films and live performances. The museum offers educational programs coordinated with school curriculum. The permanent collection also includes Gold Rush artifacts, a steam pump fire engine, a stage coach, Indian clothing, tools, railroading materials, writings of Theodore Roosevelt, and works of art.

For more information call (213) 667-2000.

Greater Los Angeles Zoo

5333 Zoo Drive, Griffith Park, Los Angeles, CA 90027-1498

GETTING THERE: Located at the junction of the Ventura Fwy (134) and the Golden State Fwy (I-5), exit either freeway at Zoo Drive.

With one of the largest animal collections in the U.S., the Los Angeles Zoo houses more than 2,000 rare and exotic animals in natural settings, including the only *zebra dinkers* in the Western Hemisphere, a Nile hippopotamus weighing three tons, and an eighteen-foot giraffe. Many interesting animals can be seen: an Arabian oryx, golden lion tamarin, Aruba Island rattlesnake, marbled cat, prettyface wallaby, and many other species, grouped into five continental areas. There is also an aquatic area, reptile house, children's zoo, alpine animal hillside, and aviary.

The two-acre children's zoo has a baby animal nursery where zoo keepers provide round-the-clock maternal care. In the baby animal compound visitors have seen infant llamas, rhinos, elephants, and camels. Miniature horses are also on view here as well as gentle barnyard animals. Be sure to visit the botanical garden and see plants from all parts of the world throughout the 113-acre site.

Educational programs include lecture tours for school groups, slide presentations, and *Zoo View* quarterly magazine. Speakers available for club meetings. Cooperative youth workshops with the California Museum of Science and Industry and with the George C. Page Museum on Saturdays for grades K-8. These include lectures, tours, films, and crafts. Also adult photography and travel programs. "World of Birds" and "Incredible Cats" shows are both entertaining and educational. Gift shop with wide range of animal-related items. Snack stands and two large picnic areas. Free parking. Wheelchair and baby stroller rental $1.50.

Open every day except Christmas, 10 A.M.–5 P.M., mid-June through August, 10 A.M.–6 P.M. An average visit takes 2–4 hours. Admission is $4.50 for adults 13 years and over, $2 for children 2–12, $3.50 for senior citizens 65 and over, children under 2 free. For more information call (213) 666-4650.

Griffith Observatory / Museum

2800 East Observatory Road, Griffith Park, Los Angeles, CA 90027

GETTING THERE: Approach Griffith Park from the Hollywood side. Take the Hollywood Fwy (U.S. 101) to Western Ave. exit. Go north on Western to Los Feliz Blvd. and east on Los Feliz to Vermont. Take Vermont north all the way to the end and connect to Observatory Road.

Situated in Griffith Park and perched atop Mt. Hollywood, the Griffith Observatory has a 650-seat planetarium theater and a Hall of Science containing over one hundred exhibits dealing with astronomy and related sciences. The daily shows in the planetarium theater are a highlight attraction. Young people especially enjoy the daily laserium shows which combine light and sound. The Foucault pendulum, a seismograph, and a six-foot earth globe will delight visitors of all ages. Occasionally there are "astronomical art" shows and "hands-on" exhibits involving a gravity well, computers, and a constellation quiz. The twelve-inch refracting telescope on the roof is open for public viewing on clear nights.

Special programs include planetarium shows, telescope workshops, fall and spring scheduled lectures. Shows held daily for school groups. Astronomy Day is held annually. Tour reservations are required. Research library for scholars, planetarium theater. Gift shop merchandise includes star charts, astronomy books, radiometers, and a "Space Stop" section offering jewelry and other gift items with space-oriented designs. Picnic area is available. Parking, ramps, wheelchair access.

Open Tuesday–Friday 2–10 P.M., Saturday 11:30 A.M.–10 P.M., Sundays and legal holidays, 12:30–10 P.M. Closed Mondays. Planetarium shows are Tuesday–Friday 3 and 8 P.M. with additional shows at 1:30, 4:30, and 8 P.M. on Saturday and Sunday. Laserium hours are Tuesday–Sunday 6:30 and 9:15 P.M. with additional shows at 10:30 P.M. Friday and Saturday. Free admission and parking. Planetarium show admission is $2.75 for 16 and older, $1.50 for children 5–15, and senior citizens 65 and older. Reservations necessary for large groups. For more information call (213) 664-1191 for a recorded message, or (213) 663-8171 for a sky information report.

Hollywood Bowl Museum

2301 Highland Ave., Los Angeles, CA 90028

GETTING THERE: Exit the Hollywood Fwy (U.S. 101) at Highland Dr. Go west to the Hollywood Bowl entrance.

Located next to the restaurant at the entrance to the Hollywood Bowl, the history of the world-famous Bowl and of the performing arts in Los Angeles is highlighted in film and beautiful major exhibitions which change yearly. Noteworthy musical instruments and all manner of memorabilia from some of the world's greatest conductors and soloists who have performed at the Bowl are featured.

A twenty-minute video documents the development of the Bowl, beginning with when it was a beautiful natural area nestled in the Hollywood mountains in 1916, the site for shooting western films. After the Los Angeles Philharmonic orchestra was formed, the site was chosen for its "Concerts Under the Stars," and a lasting tradition for Los Angeles's cultural life was begun. Celebrity performances in opera, jazz, pop, Easter sunrise services, and political rallies demonstrate the diversity of the events through the years.

Reservations necessary for tours. Audio library of historic concerts. School programs include tours of Bowl and museum. Special lectures and workshops. Interesting shop offering posters, stationery, books, records, tapes, and handcrafted jewelry. Restaurant open only during summer season. Snack bar and picnic area. Wheelchair access.

September through June open Tuesday–Saturday 9:30 A.M.–4:30 P.M. July through August open Tuesday–Sunday 9:30 A.M.–4:30 P.M. On concert nights through mid-September the museum is open until 8:30 P.M. Admission free. Parking free up until 3 P.M. on days of performance. For more information and to reserve tours, call (213) 850-2059.

Hollywood Studio Museum
2100 North Highland Ave., Hollywood, CA 90028

GETTING THERE: Take the Hollywood Fwy (U.S. 101) to the Highland Ave. exit. Go west. The museum is directly across Highland from the Hollywood Bowl entrance next to one of the Bowl parking lots at Odin St. A shuttle bus from the parking lots to the Bowl operates only during Bowl season. An underground walkway crosses Highland Ave. from Odin St.

Now a museum dedicated to silent film history, this barn-turned-movie studio is the birthplace of the Hollywood film industry. Once a ranch barn located at Selma and Vine in Hollywood, its destiny was changed when a young director, Cecil B. DeMille, rented the barn and with Jesse L. Lasky filmed *The Squaw Man*, the industry's first feature-length movie. A commercial success, the production brought credibility to a new industry and to the Jesse L. Lasky Feature Play Company.

The company continued using the barn, buying up land around it until they controlled two square blocks at Sunset and Vine. By 1926 their success forced them to move to a larger site, taking the barn with them. Through the years it was moved several times and served as a library, part of a movie set, and a gymnasium. In 1956 it was finally declared a landmark, and in 1983, with an audience of dedicated Hollywood fans watching, the barn was moved to its present site.

Displayed within are the interior of DeMille's office and a small video theater that tells the story of the film industry pioneers and DeMille's discoveries: B. B. Daniels, William S. Hart, Virginia Bruce, Marian Davies, Rudolph Valentino, Alan Hale, and Bill Boyd. The exhibition space displays large photographs and memorabilia, as well as two models of Spanish galleons used in a Douglas Fairbank's film *The Black Pirate*, the first commercial movie projector circa 1898, and the famous suit, hat and cane of Charlie Chaplin's *Tramp*.

Special programs include films, lectures, and workshops pertaining to film and to architectural preservation. Guided weekend walking tours of historic districts of Hollywood Boulevard. Call for information. Holiday party each December. Reservations required

A recreation of the 1920s office of the young director of the Jesse L. Lasky Feature Play Company, Cecil B. DeMille. Courtesy Hollywood Studio Museum.

for group tours. The gift shop sells old movie magazines, books, framed 1940s and 1950s photographs of movie stars, and some handmade dolls representing famous entertainment personalities. Picnic tables on plateau behind the barn. Wheelchair access, parking, maps.

Open Tuesday–Sunday 10 A.M.–4 P.M. Closed Mondays. Admission is $2 for adults, $1 for children, senior citizens $1.50. Parking free. For more information call (213) 874–2276.

Hollywood Wax Museum
6767 Hollywood Blvd., Los Angeles, CA 90028

GETTING THERE: Take the Hollywood Fwy (101) to Highland Ave. Go south on Highland to Hollywood Blvd. and turn left on Hollywood. Museum is between Highland and Vine.

Situated in an old movie theater near the famous Hollywood and Vine intersection, the Hollywood Museum exhibits approximately two hundred lifelike figures of famous Hollywood film stars, historical figures, and horror film characters. Smiling or peering out to visitors who walk along the darkened pathway that winds through the building, the figures grace authentic film sets. Showcased are U.S. presidents, a chillingly lifelike memorial to the astronauts of the spacecraft Challenger, likenesses of Cher, Michael Jackson, Bill Cosby, and other film notables. An entertaining section for those who like to be frightened is the "Chamber of Horrors," and for more serious aficionados of the film industry there is a film documentary of the history of the Academy Awards. Self-guided tour. The gift shops sells movie souvenirs, famous Hollywood street signs, posters, prints, and T-shirts. Neighborhood parking lots and limited street parking. Coffee shops nearby. Wheelchair access.

Open weekdays 10 A.M.–midnight, Friday and Saturday until 2 A.M. Admission for adults is $6, $5 for senior citizens over 65, juniors 13–17 $3.50, children 6–12 $4. Under 6 free. Discount of 20 percent for any group of ten or more. For more information call (213) 462–5991.

Taking an outing On Golden Pond *at the Hollywood Wax Museum. Photo by Sara LeBien.*

Travel Town Transportation Museum
5500 Zoo Drive, Los Angeles, CA 90027

GETTING THERE: The museum is near the junction of the Ventura (134) and Golden State (I-5) freeways. Exit either freeway at Zoo Drive. This leads to the entrance.

Situated in the northwest corner of Griffith Park, this is mainly an outdoor collection of trains, locomotives, trolleys, and airplanes, even a small Hawaiian sugar plantation train. Visitors can climb aboard, ride a miniature train, or visit aboard old trolleys. In addition is an enclosed museum housing a collection of vintage fire trucks.

A serious train buff may prefer to visit during the week to avoid the family crowds. Free parking. Birthday parties inside the pullman can be reserved. Call Royce & Company (818) 368-0704. Picnic tables. Food machines in the restored depot. Wheelchair access to museum.

Open weekdays 10 A.M.–5 P.M. Weekends and holidays 10 A.M.–6 P.M. Free admission. Adult fare on miniature train rides is $1.50, children $1.25, senior citizens $1, for groups of 15 or more 75¢ each. For more information call (213) 662-5874.

A train-lover's delight—The Travel Town Transportation Museum in Griffith Park. Photo by Sara LeBien.

Chapter Ten

San Fernando Valley and Antelope Valley

Andres Pico Adobe
(San Fernando Valley Historical Society)
10940 Sepulveda Blvd., Mission Hills, CA 91345

GETTING THERE: Drive north on the San Diego Fwy (I–405) to San Fernando Mission Blvd. Go east to Sepulveda Blvd. and turn right (south) to the adobe. From the Golden State Fwy (I–5) take the Brand exit, turn west to Sepulveda Blvd. The adobe is on the corner of Brand and Sepulveda. The San Fernando Mission and Lopez Adobe are other historic landmarks in close proximity.

In 1854 Andres Pico, through negotiations with his brother, Governor Pio Pico, bought an undivided one-half interest in the entire San Fernando Valley for $15,000! On this land Andres Pico built a one-room adobe, but he never liked it here, preferring instead to live in more sociable surroundings at the mission. The house changed hands several times, and by 1924 it was in disrepair when discovered by Dr. Mark Harrington, curator of the Southwest Museum and an archaeologist. When he and his wife restored it, the foundation and walls revealed some interesting historical facts about its origins. Today its furnishings and decor are typical of the late 1800s. An upstairs bedroom, converted to an exhibition hall, displays arrowhead and fossil collections, Indian rugs, tools, and quilts. Tours available. Call to reserve for groups. Museum library and archives. Educational services include films, lectures, and corn and acorn grinding demonstrations for school classes.

The annual Rancho Days event in September has a true *mercado* atmosphere with good food, craft shops, candlemaking, and more. *Las Posadas* at Christmas. The San Fernando Valley Historical

Society hosts lectures and slide programs. No gift shop. Ample picnic area on the adobe grounds. Parking. Wheelchair access to main floor.

Open Wednesday–Saturday 1–4 P.M. Closed holidays. For more information call (818) 365–7810.

Antelope Valley California Poppy Reserve
15101 West Lancaster Road, Lancaster, CA 92526

GETTING THERE: Take Antelope Valley Fwy (14) to Avenue I, turn left (west) and drive about fourteen miles. Lancaster Road is an extension of Avenue I.

This natural history museum is in the heart of the most prolific poppy-bearing land in California. During March, April, and May visitors can see breathtaking panoramas of wildflowers on the rolling hills. The Jane S. Pinheiro Interpretive Center contains 150 paintings of wildflowers by a single artist. These are of particular interest to botanists as well as backyard gardeners and floral arrangers. Special programs include a slide show and the annual California Poppy Day event on April 6. Nature hikes with docents are given during flower season. Picnic area and gift shop. Wheelchair access and parking.

Open daily from March to May 10 A.M.–4 P.M. while flowers are in bloom. Call (805) 942–0662 for flower conditions. Admission is $2 per car. Parking free. For more information call (805) 724–1180.

Antelope Valley Indian Museum
Avenue M, Lancaster, CA 93534

GETTING THERE: The museum is located in the northeast corner of Los Angeles County. Go north on Antelope Valley Fwy (14). Turn east at East Avenue J and go about seventeen miles to 150th St. Turn south to Avenue M, and left.

This anthropological and Native American Indian museum is ensconced among the rock formations of the Mojave desert and is a remarkable blend of natural rock formation and man-made structures. Even boulders form an integral part of the building. Large painted Kachina panels decorate the pitched ceiling of the main hall and other floor levels contain a Kachina Hall and the

Southwest Room. A natural passageway through the rocks leads to the spacious upper level of the house where artifacts mainly from early California Indians are arranged. Museum houses collections of Navajo rugs, Kachina dolls, basketry, beadwork, mounted animal heads, wagon wheels, primitive tools, frontier guns, and other artifacts of Native American heritage.

Films and lectures. Educational services include school visits by docents with a hands-on table and native food samples. Tours available by reservation only on Tuesday and Thursday mornings and Saturday, for groups of ten or more. Coffee shop and gift shop. Picnic area in nearby Saddleback Butte State Park. Wheelchair access.

The museum is open only on the second weekend of each month 11 A.M.–4 P.M. Closed July through September. Admission is $2 per car and includes parking fee. For more information and to reserve tours call (805) 942-0662 (State Department of Parks).

Bolton Hall Museum
10110 Commerce Ave., Tujunga, CA 91042

GETTING THERE: Travel northwest on the Foothill Fwy (I–210) to the Foothill Blvd. exit. Go east to Commerce Ave. and turn left (north) to 10110.

The history of the Sunland-Tujunga and foothill area is shown here through photographs, documents, and artifacts. It covers the period of time when a Gabrieliño Indian village was in existence, and continues through the mission and Mexican land grant periods, the development of Sunland-Tujunga, and the history of Bolton Hall. In 1913, Bolton House was a clubhouse or community center for the local families, the "Little Landers" of Tujunga. They were the followers of William Ellsworth Smythe, a philosopher, irrigationist, and social organizer. The colony disintegrated as a result of growing cynicism about their model society, but Bolton Hall continued to serve as a City Hall and as a town jail until its demise in 1957. Tours available, no reservations necessary. Annual events include entrance in the local Fourth of July Parade. Street parking. No restaurant. Wheelchair access.

Open Tuesday and Sunday 1–4 P.M. Free admission. For more information call (818) 352-3420.

Burbank's Gordon R. Howard Museum
1015 West Olive Ave., Burbank, CA 91506

GETTING THERE: Located between the Ventura (134) and Golden State (I-5) freeways. Take Olive Ave. exit from either freeway. Museum is just south of Victory Blvd. The additional two buildings are around the corner at 115 Lomita St.

Burbank was one of California's first boomtowns in the 1880s when thousands of Americans and Europeans came west on the new railroad. This beautiful museum highlights the town's development from early days to the present. Burbank's founder, Dr. David Burbank, acquired the land and developed it into farms and residential lots, with the first tract opening for sale in 1887. Prosperity came through farming, grape vineyards, the Moreland Truck Company, Burbank Studios, Lockheed Corporation, Walt Disney Studios, and real estate. These colorful exhibitions will appeal to the whole family.

In addition to historical displays, the museum complex has a vehicle collection of antique cars and a 1933 Moreland bus. A completely restored and furnished Victorian house, the Mentzer House, is also part of the complex. Tours available. Call for reservations. Christmas party at museum. Free parking in rear of park. Wheelchair access, parking and ramps.

Open Sunday 1-4 P.M. Tuesdays by reservation only for a group of ten or more. Closed on national holiday weekends. Admission is $1 for adults, free for children under 12, seniors $1. For more information call (818) 841-6333.

Casa Adobe de San Rafael
1330 Dorothy Dr., Glendale, CA 91202

GETTING THERE: From Ventura Fwy (134) take the Pacific exit and go north on Pacific to Stocker. Go right on Stocker, left on Dorothy, and continue north to the adobe.

Tucked behind a high wall of adobe brick, among tall trees and blooming magnolias, camellias, orange trees heavy with fruit, and birds of paradise, is the lovely Casa Adobe de San Rafael—a tranquil Spanish-style oasis in a landscape of apartment buildings and neighborhood homes. Built in 1865 by Thomas and Maria Sanchez, this old house is furnished with elegant nineteenth-century

Casa Adobe de San Raphael—a step back in time. Photo by Sara LeBien.

furniture, oriental rugs, and hanging lamps. Free parking. Picnic tables. Wheelchair access on grounds and in house.

Grounds open daily 8 A.M.-dusk. Museum is open from the last week of June to the first week of September, 1–4 P.M. Open by appointment only 10–10:30 A.M. during winter. Closed Mondays and Tuesdays. For more information and to reserve tours call (818) 244-4651.

Casa de Geronimo Lopez/Lopez Adobe
1100 Pico St., San Fernando, CA 91340

GETTING THERE: The museum is located at the corner of Maclay and Pico streets, between the Foothill (210) and Golden State (I–5) freeways. From 210 take the Maclay exit and go west past Glen Oaks and Truman to Pico. From I–5 take the Brand or Mission exit and go about 1 mile east to Pico. Turn right to Maclay.

Geronimo Lopez began the first post office in the San Fernando Valley and was the first postmaster. He built this house in 1882. His wife wanted a fine Victorian-style house, but knowing it would be uncomfortably warm in the California summers, Lopez built the two-story house with twenty-four-inch thick adobe. Stagecoach travelers called the house "Lopez Station" and stopped here en route to San Francisco. Furnished in the Victorian period of the 1890s, it displays traditional furniture and clothing. The rooms are changed seasonally to include holiday decor of the era. Annual events include the blessing of fruits and flowers on the first Sunday in June, and a Christmas tour. Wheelchair access available only on first floor. Tours.

Open Wednesday–Saturday 11 A.M.–3 P.M., Sunday 1–4 P.M. Free admission and parking. For more information call (818) 361-7542 and (818) 361-5050.

The Doctor's House
1601 West Mountain St., Glendale, CA 91201

GETTING THERE: Adjacent to the Brand Library in Brand Park. From the Golden State Fwy (I–5) take the Western (east) exit. Go two blocks to Western and turn north. Follow Western to Mountain St.

This two-story Victorian home was the residence and office of three prominent Glendale physicians between 1895 and 1914. Built around 1888 in Queen Anne-Eastgate style, it was one of the more fashionable houses in the area. When inevitable growth and change came to Glendale the house was doomed to demolition, but the city of Glendale and Glendale Historical Society stepped in to preserve and restore the house and surrounding gardens to its original Victorian splendor. Restoration has been extensive, including repairing and remilling the three Moongate-Arch porches and reproducing lost items after searching early photographs. The doctors' office still displays reproductions of medical equipment, lighting fixtures, and other Victorian era fittings.

Annual exhibit of antique Christmas ornaments. Wheelchair access, family picnic area, free parking.

Open for guided tours on Sundays 2–4 P.M. Group tours Monday–Saturday with reservations. Free admission. Closed on major holiday weekends. For more information call (818) 243–8204.

Forest Lawn Memorial-Parks (Glendale)
1712 South Glendale Ave., Glendale, CA 91205

GETTING THERE: Take Ventura Fwy (134) east to Glendale Ave. Go south 1½ miles to entrance. Buses, trailers, or recreational vehicles are restricted. No bicycles or motorcycles without special permission.

A cemetery might not usually be thought of as a museum, but *millions* of visitors come to Forest Lawn Memorial Park each year to see its captivating art treasures and stroll through its beautiful grounds. A well-illustrated map and guide assist visitors in locating the paintings and outdoor statuary which include exact reproductions of many of Michelangelo's most famous works.

A popular landmark at Forest Lawn is the Hall of the Crucifixion-Resurrection, housing the world's largest oil paintings, *The Crucifixion* by Jan Styka and *The Resurrection* by Robert Clark. Next to the hall is a museum of decorative and fine arts and historical objects. A highlight for Michelangelo devotees is *The Sotterraneo*, an exact replica of an underground room in the Medici Chapel in Florence, Italy, believed to be where Michelangelo hid for ninety-two days in 1530 during a political upheaval which threatened his life. While confined to the 9-by-33-foot room he drew fifty-six

181

sketches on the walls. Later the walls were whitewashed and forgotten for 445 years, but in 1975 the room and drawings were discovered. It may be the most significant artistic discovery of this century.

A display of bronzes includes Jean Antoine Houdon's full-size bronze of George Washington, Gladys Lewis-Bush's bronze of Mark Twain, and James Earle Fraser's bust of Theodore Roosevelt, and many other works. There are also original works (or their reproductions) of Harriet Whitney Frishmuth, Enzo Pasquini, L. Villanis and Adolph Alexander Weinman, Henri Weigel, Andrea Del Verrocchio, and Leone Tommasi.

The Hans Christian Anderson exhibit displays a priceless collection of his original manuscripts, and early editions, illustrations, and miniatures of his works. In addition, a large exhibition features a complete collection of antiquity coins. *The Paradise Doors*, a copy of Rodin's bronze cast *Gates of Paradise*, which can be found at the Baptistry of St. John in Florence, Italy, is displayed on floor level, permitting visitors to easily see the magnificent detail of religious story panels. Tour reservations are required for groups. The gift shop offers a limited selection of religious items. No eating facilities. Wheelchair access. Free parking.

Open daily 10 A.M.–5 P.M. No charge for admission. For more information call (818) 241-4151.

William S. Hart Ranch and Museum
2415 Newhall Ave., Newhall, CA 91322

GETTING THERE: Take Golden State Fwy (I–5) to the Antelope Valley Fwy (14) to the San Fernando Valley Road exit and follow it to the entrance.

This 260-acre county park was once the home of the popular western actor and film director, William Surrey Hart. A great silent film star, Hart made his first film in 1914 and went on to make seventy films in the next eleven years. During that time he lived on this 264-acre ranch, then named *La Loma de Los Vientos* (The Hill of the Winds), where he entertained his friends in a large two-story Spanish mansion. It remains much as it was, furnished with his personal possessions, sketches, and paintings by close friends

Charles Russell and Frederic Remington, and housing bronzes, guns, and movie memorabilia throughout the property.

When Hart died in 1946 the Los Angeles County Department of Parks and Recreation converted the estate into a recreational park. Restoration is taking place in the bunkhouse, ranch house, and corrals. Other features include a dog cemetery and a shed housing early farming equipment. Children will enjoy the winding footpath to the hilltop museum mansion. Guided tour. Annual events include a Fourth of July Parade which begins at the ranch and a Western Jamboree in September featuring well-known Nashville musicians. Docents dressed in western apparel travel to schools with a "Cowboy Trunk" full of ropes, branding iron, horseshoes, saddle, stories of local and western history and cowboy lore. Free parking. Ample picnic area. Wheelchair access and special parking.

The park is open daily 10 A.M.-dusk, June 15–October 1. The museum is open Wednesday–Friday 10 A.M.–5 P.M. and Saturday and Sunday 10 A.M.–4:30 P.M. Closed on New Year's Day, Thanksgiving and Christmas. From October 1–June 15, tours are Wednesday–Friday 10 A.M.–1 P.M. and on Saturday and Sunday 11 A.M.–4 P.M. No admission fees, but donations are appreciated. For more information call (805) 259-0855.

Leonis Adobe and Plummer House

23537 Calabasas Road, Calabasas, CA 91302

GETTING THERE: Take Ventura Fwy (U.S. 101) west to the Mulholland and Valley Circle exit. Go over the freeway overpass and turn right on Calabasas Road. Coming from the west, turn right at the freeway exit and continue into Calabasas.

One of four adobes in the San Fernando Valley still in existence, this was the home of a shrewd, tenacious landowner, Miguel Leonis, who controlled and ruled over the west end of the valley in the 1800s, earning the title "King of Calabasas." A Monterey-style mansion, the adobe is furnished in the 1875 period. Visitors will notice protruding nails along the upstairs hall, used for hanging grapes to dry into raisins. Upstairs also is a copper-lined, walnut-paneled bathtub, and outside is a large Mexican beehive oven used to bake bread and meat, and a tank house used for wine making. In addition are a furnished barn, windmill, watertower, gardens, and farm animals.

Recreated "pantry" and table setting at the Leonis Adobe. Photo by Sara LeBien.

The Plummer House, built in 1878 on Rancho La Brea (the site of the La Brea tar pits), is also located here. Beautifully restored, it now serves as a museum with displays on the history of Calabasas. Tours available for schools and the general public. Call for reservations. A modest selection of gifts and books in the museum shop. Picnic area on the grounds. Restaurants are within the immediate block. Free parking, wheelchair access.

Open Wednesday–Sunday 1–4 P.M. Donations are accepted. For more information call (818) 712-0734.

Los Angeles Valley College Historical Museum
5800 Fulton Ave., Van Nuys, CA 91401

GETTING THERE: Take the Hollywood Fwy (170) north to Burbank or Oxnard. Turn left (west) and go to Fulton Ave. The campus lies between Burbank and Oxnard, Fulton and Coldwater Canyon. From the Ventura Fwy (U.S. 101) take the Coldwater Canyon exit north to campus.

Housed in a small bungalow on the campus of Los Angeles Valley College, this museum specializes in artifacts and documents on the history of the San Fernando Valley. There are also exhibits of large collections of 1920s clothing, geological findings from the Santa Monica mountains, and documentary material relating to William Paul Whitsett, founder of Van Nuys. Tours available. Limited college parking; street parking. No eating facilities or wheelchair access.

Open Monday–Friday 1–4 P.M. during the school year. Closed holidays. Free admission. For more information call (818) 781-1200, ext. 373.

Los Encinos State Historical Park
16756 Moorpark St., Encino, CA 91316

GETTING THERE: Take the Ventura Fwy (U.S. 101) to the Balboa Blvd. exit. Go south to Moorpark St., about ½ block before Ventura. Turn left on Moorpark to the park entrance.

Busy, congested Ventura Boulevard in the San Fernando Valley, once called *El Camino Real*, was the principal coastal route north to San Francisco. The Butterfield Mail Line traveled this road and one of its water stops was at the *Rancho del Encino* ("Oak Ranch"), an adobe-style house built in 1849 on a cattle ranch of 4,460 acres. Individual travelers on horseback or by carriage also stopped here to drink from the lake or to spend the night. A historic landmark now, the nine rooms display popular pieces of the 1800s typical of the successful ranch families of that era. A hair couch, lace tablecloths, and the original bedroom furniture are well worth seeing. The museum's ongoing Living History programs demonstrate sheep shearing, food preparation, candle dipping, blacksmithing, clothes washing, and games from the 1870s. Tours for schools, special groups, and general public. Annual events include "Victorian Christmas," and "1870's Ranching Life."

The natural, spring-fed lake-reservoir on the park grounds is an attraction for many birds and ducks. Tours offered Wednesday–Sunday 1 P.M.–4 P.M. 50¢ for adults, $.25 for children 6–17. A few books on California history, native plants and birds available in gift shop. There are restaurants in the Encino area along Ventura Blvd., and ample picnic area on the adobe grounds. Wheelchair access. Free parking is limited to five cars. Limited street parking.

Museum grounds are open Wednesday–Sunday 8 A.M.–5 P.M. The house is open 1–4 P.M. Admission to the grounds is free, and there is a minimal charge for the house tour. For more information call (818) 784-4849.

Merle Norman Classic Beauty Collections at San Sylmar
15180 Bledsoe St., Sylmar, CA 91342

GETTING THERE: Take the Golden State Fwy (I–5) north. Sylmar is about twenty-five miles north of Los Angeles. Take the first Roxford St. exit and turn right on Roxford St., right on San Fernando Road, and left on Bledsoe St.

The name of this museum is deceptive. Do they display antique cosmetics? No, no bottles and jars here. This collection includes one of the world's most outstanding displays of classic and antique automobiles as well as hundreds of rare mechanical musical instruments.

The elegant interior of this building was designed to imitate the glamorous car shows of the 1930s, and the ceilings are glazed with

Costing $20,000 in 1933, this elegant Duesenberg Torpedo Sedan is the centerpiece of the Merle Norman Classic Beauty Collections at San Sylmar. Courtesy of museum.

gold leaf. The major exhibitions are in three areas: the Grand Salon, the Music Room, and a gallery. The Salon, a formal marble-pillared showroom, features priceless antique luxury cars. One is an award-winning Duesenberg Torpedo Sedan, designed for the 1933 World's Fair in Chicago, and Rudolph Valentino's 1923 Avions Voisin is also here.

The Music Room houses an astonishing collection of antique music boxes, phonographs, and mechanical music instruments. A rare collection of massive "orchestrations," large mechanical instruments that imitate an orchestra and a musical watch collection are also featured. The mezzanine above the Grand Salon displays a collection of 1,100 hood ornaments, some of which are Lalique crystal, and silver and crystal "mascots" which served as radiator caps. Street parking. Wheelchair access and ramps.

Reservations are necessary well in advance for admission. Open to adults, children 12 and older only. Admission free. For more information and to make reservations call (818) 367-2251.

Mission San Fernando Rey de España
15151 San Fernando Mission Blvd., Mission Hills, CA 91345

GETTING THERE: The museum is located on San Fernando Mission Blvd., accessible from both the San Diego (I-405) and the Golden State (I-5) freeways.

For anyone interested in California history this mission gives an excellent picture of daily life in the early mission chain. Mission San Fernando was founded by Padre Fermin Lasuen in 1797, and the beautiful chapel is still used on Sunday mornings. An exact replica of the earlier edifice built between 1804 and 1806, its walls are seven feet thick at the base and it houses the original church furnishings. A small cemetery immediately behind the chapel was for the early settlers, and their names are still visible on the gravestones. In the large, gothic-shaped mission are facsimile settings of the leather craftsmen, weavers, potters, and blacksmiths. The *convento* was completed in 1822, and its long corridor of small rooms display magnificent altar furnishings, vestments, and religious art. Collections also include Spanish furnishings, seventeenth- and eighteenth-century *santos*, altar settings, vestments, relief panels, basketry, and religious art.

Beyond the chapel is the Archival Center for the Archdiocese of Los Angeles. Its main function is to preserve and interpret documents, manuscripts, and other historical information about the Catholic church. Western art, Papal medals, and mission and Vatican memorabilia are on view here. The Archival Center is open to the public only on Monday and Thursday from 1 P.M.–3 P.M. Educational materials are available for teachers. Library open by appointment. Gift shop carries adult and juvenile books about early California and the missions, large selection of religious gifts, posters, statuary, and creche figures. No restaurants. Free parking nearby. Wheelchair access.

Open daily 9 A.M.–5 P.M. No admittance after 4:15 P.M. Admission $1 for adults, 50¢ for children, under 7 free. For more information call (818) 365-1501.

NASA Ames-Dryden Research Center and Flight Museum

P.O. Box 273, Edwards Air Force Base, Edwards, California 93523

GETTING THERE: The museum is located on Edwards Air Force Base, about 2½ hours northeast of Los Angeles. Take Golden State Fwy (I-5) north to Antelope Valley Fwy (14), then north to Lancaster. Follow signs to Edwards AFB. Visitors to base must show proof of insurance, driver's license, and current vehicle registration.

This small museum houses impressive exhibitions explaining the Center's aeronautical research. Exhibits elaborate on the Center's techniques for solving such problems as aerodynamic heating and stability and control effectiveness at high speeds and altitudes. Space suits and test pilot pressure suits are also on display, including the Apollo space suit worn on the moon. Other permanent exhibitions include beautiful, large oil paintings on aeronautical themes, as well as models of the lunar landing research vehicle, a Boeing 747, and the Space Shuttle Orbiter. An introductory film and one and one-half hour tour is offered at 10:15 A.M. and 1:15 P.M. Reservations required only for groups. No flashcubes or flashbars permitted. An annual event is the Air Force open house and air show in September or October. The gift shop sells quality items of aircraft design, including commemoratives. Cafeteria. Free parking. Wheelchair access.

Open weekdays 7:45 A.M.–3:45 P.M. Closed weekends, holidays, and during shuttle operations. Admission is free. For more information call (805) 258-3311.

Placerita Canyon Nature Center
19152 Placerita Canyon Road, Newhall, CA 91321

GETTING THERE: Go north on the San Diego Fwy (I–405) or Golden State Fwy (I–5) to Antelope Valley Fwy (14). Continue on 14 to the Placerita Canyon exit, turn right, and go about two miles to the entrance.

A small gem tucked in a beautiful canyon, this nature museum has first-rate exhibits. Its displays center around the local environment, rocks, geological faults, fire ecology, microclimates, weather, animals, reptiles, and birds. From smog to spiderwebs, rattlesnakes to woodpeckers, the displays are educational and very accessible. There is even a dinner table set with edible leaves and seeds which may interest hikers.

Unlike most museums, the interesting labels are placed low enough for children and wheelchair users to appreciate. Educational programs include lectures, workshops, weekly live animal presentations, school programs. The museum also maintains a rehabilitation service for injured birds. Surrounded by 350 acres of hiking and equestrian trails. Heritage Trail reveals some of the history of the canyon, which was the site of the first major gold strike in California. Alliklik Indian history and a family cabin from the early 1900s with remains of drilling equipment are also marked on trails. Ask for self-guided tour brochure. There is also a wheelchair path through a scented plant grove with labels in braille. Gift shop. Picnic area. Free parking, wheelchair access.

Open daily 9 A.M.–5 P.M. Closed Thanksgiving, Christmas, and New Year's Day. Free admission. For more information call (805) 259-7721.

Southern Pacific Train Depot and Museum of Saugus
24107 San Fernando Road, Newhall, CA 91321

GETTING THERE: Take Golden State (I–5) to the Antelope Valley Fwy (14), then north to San Fernando Road. Follow signs to the driveway entrance right before the entrance to the William S. Hart Park, an adjoining property.

The Placerita Canyon Nature Center Museum doctors up more than 260 injured birds a year, in addition to teaching about the local environment. Photo by Sara LeBien.

Once a very busy Southern Pacific train depot in Saugus in 1910, this building was saved from demolition by the endeavors of the Santa Clarita Valley Historical Society, whose members raised $60,000 to move it, in the dead of the night, to the present site in nearby Newhall. A true-to-life display of the railroad and the agent's office has 1910 furnishings, train timetables, lanterns, a crank telephone, and telegraph key. Santa Clarita Valley history is displayed in the former baggage room, where furnishings, circa 1910, and local history artifacts from homes, stores, gold fields, and farms are on display. Travel cases believed to have belonged to Belle Starr and Mark Twain, and the Estay Organ once belonging to the composer of "I Love You Truly" are part of the eclectic collection. Old general store items, Indian grinding stones, and a realistic diorama of a placer mining scene are also shown. Annual events include an "Old Town" celebration featuring horseshoeing, crafts, square dancing, stagecoach rides, and old-style picturetaking. Special programs for schools and community groups. The gift shop displays Santa Clarita Historical Society publications and stationery, cookbooks, and train whistles. No eating facilities. Wheelchair access and ramps. Free parking.

Open Sunday 2–4 P.M. No admission fees, but donations are appreciated. For more information call (805) 254–1275.

Chapter Eleven

Thousand Oaks North to Santa Barbara and Goleta

Albinger Archaeological Museum

113 East Main St., Ventura, CA 93003

GETTING THERE: From the Ventura Fwy (U.S. 101) take the California St. exit north to Main St. and turn west. Continue three blocks. The museum is across the street from the Ventura County Historical Museum.

In 1973 the buildings which stood here were demolished as part of an urban redevelopment program, but archaeological studies revealed important artifacts of 3,500 years of history below the soil. During 1974–75 the extensive digs uncovered more than 30,000 artifacts representing five distinct periods of human settlement here: prehistoric, Chumash, Spanish, Mexican, and Anglo-pioneer. Now withdrawn from any redevelopment plan, the site is on the National Historic Register. A ten-minute presentation on artifacts and the former residents of the site is featured along with several exposed archaeological foundations outside, including the remains of a "lost mission church" and an ancient oven. Films, free lectures, tours available. Reservations not required. Annual events include "Archaeology Day" on the second Saturday of November. Christmas open house on the first Sunday in December. City parking lot across the street. Wheelchair access, special parking.

Open Tuesday–Sunday 10 A.M.–4 P.M. Closed Mondays. Free admission and parking. For more information call (805) 648–5823.

Carnegie Art Museum
424 South C St., Oxnard, CA 93930

GETTING THERE: The museum is located between 4th and 5th streets, three blocks west of Oxnard Blvd. From the north on Ventura Fwy (U.S. 101), take the Oxnard Blvd. exit east to 4th St. Turn right and go to C St. From the south, take the Vineyard exit. Go left over the bridge, and turn left at the intersection of Oxnard Blvd. and Vineyard Ave. Turn right on 4th St. and go to C St.

With its permanent collection concentrating on California art from 1924 to the present, the Carnegie also offers traveling exhibitions surveying a broad range of art such as Japanese photography of the 1800s and works by contemporary Italian sculptor, Franco Giuti.

In the permanent collection are paintings by Cornelius Botke, Arthur Edwaine Beaumont, Jessie Arms Botke, Colin Campbell Cooper, Ejnar Hansen, Emil Jean Kosa Jr., Paul Lauritz and Kathryn Woodman Leighton. This Municipal Art Collection had its beginning in 1925 when the Oxnard Art Club was formed and began its tradition of donating a painting per year to the city. Last year a new public subscription program for acquiring works of art for the museum was introduced.

A permanent gallery for the collection was realized in 1980 with the renovation of the Carnegie Building, one of over a thousand similar structures built by philanthropist Andrew Carnegie as public libraries. Built in 1906 the original columns still surround the entrance, and a chandelier of the same period graces the interior. Reopened in 1980 as the Carnegie Cultural Arts Center, the building houses the municipal collection and provides space for the Historical Society Museum and the Art Club of Oxnard.

A wide range of educational programs are offered including lectures on art history, contemporary art, and art techniques and theories. Also art classes, art-related travel tours, and slide presentations from the National Gallery of Art extension service. Lecture series of noteworthy topics such as "Greek Archaeology," "Art Conservation for Collectors and Artists," and "Women Artists of California Impressionism." School tours. Library open to public.

Carnegie Art Museum concentrates on the contemporary. Here paintings by Dickens Chang and sculpture by Franco Ciuti. Courtesy of museum.

Call or write for yearly exhibition schedule. No gift shop. Picnic area in nearby park. Wheelchair access. Free parking.

Open Tuesday–Saturday 10 A.M.–5 P.M. Free admission. For more information call (805) 984-4649.

Carpinteria Valley Museum of History
956 Maple Ave., Carpinteria, CA 93013

GETTING THERE: Take Ventura Fwy (U.S. 101) to the Casitas Pass Road exit. Go west to Carpinteria Ave. Turn right to Maple Ave.

Although the objects in this museum are old, the museum has an up-to-date vitality in educational development. Changing exhibits, school programs, festivals, summer projects, and an oral history program indicate that the study of local history is alive and well in Carpinteria.

The museum features permanent and changing exhibits on the culture of the Chumash Indians, Spanish-Mexicans, Anglo-pioneers, and Victorian periods of early California. There are also a few creative displays pertaining to the world-renowned lima bean production here prior to the development of avocado and citrus. Selected from the museum's collection of 4,600 photographs of local history, several wall-size enlargements of antique photographs which have been hand-tinted in oils show early agriculture techniques. Off-shore oil drilling history is displayed in murals. An extensive American Indian collection includes items for body adornment, bone tools for basket weaving, whale rib bone, implements, ceremonial objects, and reproductions of original Chumash Indian rock art. The latter were painted by Campbell Grant, the definitive Chumash rock art expert and author who happens to be a Carpinteria resident. A turn-of-the-century schoolroom and blacksmith shop are also represented. Annual events include spring lecture series, a "Summer Faire," an oral history project, Potluck Picnic, and "Holiday Faire." School tours, outreach programs, summer program, research assistance, oral history tapes, photographic collection. Library. Tours available. Call for reservations. Street parking. Gift shop. No restaurants. Wheelchair access.

Open weekdays 1:30–4 P.M., Saturday 11 A.M.–4 P.M., Sunday 1:30–4 P.M. Free admission. For more information call (805) 684-3112.

CEC/Seabee Museum

U.S. Naval Construction Battalion Center, Port Hueneme, CA 93043

GETTING THERE: From the Ventura Fwy (U.S. 101) take the Wagon Wheel exit. Turn west onto Ventura Road. Follow southward to the Sunkist Road gate of the naval center where the museum sign is posted.

Probably very few people know that there is a museum at the U.S. Construction Naval Battalion Center in Point Hueneme, and also that it is well worth the drive from Los Angeles. All manner of historical and contemporary weapons, uniforms, models, and personal effects are on display. Detailed dioramas depict the Seabees in various operations as well as show underwater construction techniques and a model of a civil engineering laboratory on the ocean floor.

The ceiling is hidden by a mass of colorful flags—all worn, some tattered—brought back by Seabee units stationed in various countries around the world. The interesting cultural memorabilia wing displays tools, weapons, currency, clothing, musical instruments, and dolls from many parts of the world where the Seabees served. Films and lectures regularly offered. Annual events include memorial service in museum memorial chapel. Research library. Guided tours offered infrequently and by reservation. Gift shop sells souvenirs, T-shirts and jewelry. Picnic area. Wheelchair access and parking. Free parking.

Open Monday–Friday 8 A.M.–4:30 P.M., Saturday 9 A.M.–4:30 P.M. and Sunday 12:30–4:30 P.M. Closed holidays. Admission free. To receive a visitor's pass you must show a driver's license and car registration at the entrance gate. For more information call (805) 982-5163.

Channel Islands National Park

1901 Spinnaker Dr., Ventura, CA 93001

GETTING THERE: From Ventura Fwy (U.S. 101) north, take the Victoria Ave. exit south. Follow Olivas Park Dr. west into Spinnaker Dr. From U.S. 101 southbound take the Seaward Ave. exit and go south to Harbor Blvd. Turn west on Shoreline Dr., which becomes Spinnaker Dr.

Channel Islands National Park Visitors Center is a fine maritime and coastal museum. Photo by Sara LeBien.

The visitors center in this national park is really a fine small museum. Photographs introduce a general overview of the plant and animal life of the Channel Islands, and simulated seashore exhibits. An indoor tidepool is encrusted with numerous live anemones, sea urchins, crabs, starfish, and plant life. An underwater interpretive program on video and a film on the ecology of the islands are available. Chumash Indian artifacts are also displayed. Lectures and outdoor programs are regularly scheduled during the summer on Friday and Saturday evening and Sunday afternoon. Annual events include "Celebration of the Whale" and "Environmental Fair." School tours and programs for special groups such as diving and yacht clubs. Theatre and observation tower on premises. Gift shop sells books on Chumash Indians, seashore and marine life, natural history, and videos and cassettes on the Channel Islands. Delicatessen next door in the marina. Wheelchair access, elevator to tower.

Open daily 8 A.M.–5 P.M. Free admission and parking. For more information call (805) 644-8464 or (805) 644-8262.

Conejo Valley Art Museum
191 West Wilbur Road, Thousand Oaks, CA 91360

GETTING THERE: From the Ventura Fwy (U.S. 101) take the Moorpark Road exit and go north on Moorpark to Hillcrest. Turn left and proceed to Wilbur. Turn right.

When the Conejo Valley Art Museum was looking for a new home, the city of Thousand Oaks invited them to occupy part of the former Conejo Library building. The structure's high-pitched roofline and skylights lends itself well as an exhibition gallery. As this young museum is developing a permanent collection it celebrates a diversity of artistic expression, from exhibits of Navajo weaving, serigraphy of the fifties, and Japanese architectural design, to tribal expressions of Africa and New Guinea and an exhibit of quilts by contemporary artists. For museum-goers in the northwest section of San Fernando Valley, Westlake and Conejo Valley, this museum is becoming a significant art center. An Art Rental Gallery loans original art for business and home. The museum also offers free lectures, films, and live demonstrations. Annual events include a juried photography show and exhibits with western American themes to coincide with the festivities of the annual Conejo Days.

The Conejo Valley Art Museum offers contrasts and diversity. Photo by Sara LeBien.

Classes in art appreciation and studio. School tours. The gift shop has an international selection of handmade art objects, jewelry, books, handmade paper, baskets, and pottery. No restaurants. Wheelchair access.

Open Wednesday–Sunday noon–5 P.M. Free admission and parking. For more information call (805) 373–0054.

Fillmore Historical Museum
447 Main St., Fillmore, CA 93015

GETTING THERE: Fillmore is between Magic Mountain and Ventura County. From the Ventura Fwy (U.S. 101), take Route 126 north to Central Ave. exit. Continue north on Central to Main St. and turn right.

Nearly all of the household furnishings, clothing, and art collectibles in this museum were from homes in the Fillmore area. An early music box with its forty-two discs is played for visitors, and the kitchen and bedroom depict everyday life in the 1900s through 1920s. Period photographs are on exhibit as well as a rare collection of orange crate labels acquired from the early years of the local citrus packing houses. Tours available, reservations necessary. The gift shop sells old citrus labels and reproductions, T-shirts, photographic reproductions of historic Fillmore. No wheelchair facilities.

Open Tuesday–Sunday 1–4:30 P.M. Closed Mondays. Free admission. Limited free parking. For more information call (805) 524–0948.

Goleta Depot Railroad Museum
300 North Los Carneros Road, Goleta, CA 93117

GETTING THERE: Take the Ventura Fwy (U.S. 101) north to the Los Carneros Road exit. The museum is one block north.

Through the efforts of community volunteers the old Goleta Depot was saved and moved to this site. Many of the displayed artifacts and photographs reflect the days when the depot was a Southern Pacific train station. The ground level of the building shows the agent's office with a working telegraph and other communication equipment. Hands-on exhibitions in the waiting room complement an interesting slide presentation. In the freight room is an elaborate

Antique citrus labels are now a collector's item. The Fillmore Historical Society Museum gift shop has other interesting reproductions of memorabilia.

HO layout, including the depot, railroad yards, train, and local topography, showing the route of the former Southern Pacific train service. The former agent's living quarters upstairs now house the bookstore and the office of the Institute for American Research which operates the museum.

Tours available. Reservations required for groups. The third Sunday of October is "Depot Day," an open house and barbecue, and tracks are put down for a small steamer train. A Christmas party with a toy train display is held the last three Saturdays of December. Educational services include lectures and railroad excursions for children. Gift shop sells train-related books. No restaurant. Wheelchair access.

Open Monday–Saturday 1–4 P.M. Free admission and parking. For more information call (805) 964-3540.

Mission Santa Barbara
Laguna St. and Los Olivas, Santa Barbara, CA 93105

GETTING THERE: Located on the upper end of Laguna St. Take Ventura Fwy (U.S. 101) to State St. or Santa Barbara St. Go toward the mountains to Mission St. Turn right on Mission and follow to Laguna.

The original structure, built in 1786, was California's tenth founded mission, and was later destroyed by an earthquake. The present building was dedicated in 1820, and is still an active church. A self-guided tour explores the original missionary living quarters. Today they contain beautiful displays of artifacts, diagrams, and photos relating to mission history. One bedroom displays an early telescope and the kitchen is equipped with a large double oven. Gregorian chants are played throughout the mission's museum area. Last on the tour is the chapel, painted in mute tones of green and pink, with a high ceiling and dark beams softly lighted by a large iron chandelier. Many works of eighteenth- and nineteenth-century Mexican art are here along with two large religious paintings approximately two centuries old. The surrounding gardens and cemetery where over 4,000 Indian converts are buried, as well as early vaults, are well worth exploring. Gift shop sells religious items. No restaurant. Wheelchair access, free parking.

The Mission Santa Barbara is a lovely retreat from a hectic life-style. Photo by Sara LeBien.

Open daily 9 A.M.–5 P.M. Admission is $1 for adults, children under 16 free. Be sure to pick up the brochure map at the visitor's bureau; it shows many local historic sites. For more information call (805) 682-4713.

Ojai Valley Museum and Historical Society
109 South Montgomery St., Ojai, CA 93023

GETTING THERE: From Ventura Fwy (U.S. 101), take Ventura Road (33) to Ojai. Follow Ojai Ave. to Montgomery and turn north.

The museum is one block from Main St. and next to the Art Center. This tiny museum is housed in the old fire station and features local history. The colorful exhibits and artifacts are artistically installed and illustrate the life of early Indians and also the development of oil and agriculture interests in the Ojai Valley. Excavations in its vicinity have determined that the Chumash Indians lived here 2,000 to 3,000 years ago and that the Oak Grove tribes had been here 3,000 to 7,000 years before that. A basketry collection showcases the skills of the early West Coast Indians. A reproduced ranchhouse with Victorian furnishings is also on the premises. Other exhibits are on natural history and fossils and there is a popular tidepool exhibit. Tours available by reservation. Films and lectures regularly offered. Library on premises. School tours. Gift shop. No restaurant. Wheelchair parking in rear, access to first floor.

Open Wednesday–Monday 1–5 P.M. Closed Tuesdays. Free admission and parking. Donations appreciated. For more information and to reserve tours call (805) 646-2290.

Old Spanish Days Carriage Museum
129 Castillo St., Santa Barbara, CA 93101

GETTING THERE: Take Ventura Fwy (U.S. 101) north to Santa Barbara. Exit at Castillo and turn toward the ocean. The museum is adjacent to Pershing Park sports field, approximately one block west of Castillo St.

In this modest, inconspicuous building is housed a wonderful, elaborate collection of sixty antique horse-drawn carriages and a display of beautiful saddles and tack.

The title of the museum is a misnomer, since the carriages are not all Spanish but mainly American, and they include an old circus bandwagon, a Phaeton carriage, a six-seat bronson wagon (circa 1880), a doctor's house-calling buggy, an elegant Italian carriage with large handsome carriage lamps, and an enormous fifteen-seat mountain buggy similar to those used for sightseeing tours in Yosemite. These carriages and buggies are in excellent condition. Many are unusual and even rare, and are used in the annual "Old Spanish Days Fiesta" held in the first week of August. A rare piece in the collection, dated 1648, is a massive hand-carved wagon for transporting wine barrels. Every inch is carved with figures, faces, flowers, and leaves. There is a collection of forty-seven saddles, including Will Rogers's, Clark Gable's, and the Cisco Kid's, displayed along with roping saddles, side-saddles, children's, ladies, working, and parade saddles, and an equally extensive display of stirrups and bridles. School tours available. Attendants on hand to answer questions or conduct unstructured tour. Picnic area. Wheelchair access.

Open Sunday 2–4 P.M. Free admission and parking. Donations appreciated. For information call (805) 962-2353.

Olivas Adobe Historical Park
4200 Olivas Park Dr., Ventura, CA 93002

GETTING THERE: Take Ventura Fwy (U.S. 101) north to the Victoria Ave. exit. Go south to Olivas Park Dr.

The land on which this adobe was built was part of the vast landholding of the Mission San Buenaventura in 1782. After the Secularization Act in 1833, the Mexican government granted a parcel to Raimundo Olivas and Felipe Lorenzana, requiring certain improvements, such as building a house, raising cattle, and planting grain, fruit trees, and grapevines. Raimundo's family built the original small adobe and lived here until 1879. This Monterey-style adobe faces a spacious courtyard bordered by massive 120-year-old eucalyptus trees. Inside, the house is as handsomely furnished as it would have been in the 1870s, including the original barrel mechanical piano and an upstairs chapel.

Max Fleischmann, of the Fleischmann Yeast and Margarine Company, was the final resident of the house. He used it as a

"Old Adobe Days" *attracts spectators and performers to Olivas Adobe Historical* *Park.* *Courtesy of museum.*

duck-hunting lodge and frequently entertained celebrities here. Lectures, workshops, and plays are currently offered on the premises. Annual events include "Old Adobe Days," in the summer, with live music, craft and nineteenth-century domestic demonstrations. The beautiful, candlelit "Christmas Posada" is a nativity play presented each Christmas Eve. Educational services include outreach programs relating Native American and rancho life as well as natural history. Hands-on programs. Group tours available during the week with reservations two weeks in advance. Picnic area. Wheelchair access.

Open Saturday and Sunday 10 A.M.–4 P.M. Free admission and parking. For more information call (805) 644-4346.

Ortega Adobe
215 West Main St., Ventura, CA 93001

GETTING THERE: Take Ventura Fwy (U.S. 101) to California St. exit. Go north to Main St. Turn left.

Typical of the adobes along Santa Barbara's Main Street in the 1800s this home was built by Emigdio Ortega and reflects the Spanish-Mexican heritage of this region. Timbers were hauled in by oxcart all the way from Fillmore, and discarded tiles were purchased from the mission. Of the eight children raised here, one son, Emilio, later started the first commercial food operation in California—the Ortega Chili Company. The simple adobe rooms may be viewed through girded windows and doorways. True-to-life dramatizations of early adobe life are featured on occasion. Tours available. Reservations required for groups. Walking tour guidebooks are available at the museum and city hall and list all nearby historic sites. Free parking. Limited wheelchair access.

Open daily 9 A.M.–4 P.M. For more information call the Ventura County Museum of History and Art, at (805) 653-0323 or (805) 648-5823.

Port Hueneme Historical Museum
Hueneme Road and Market St., Port Hueneme, CA 93043

GETTING THERE: From the Ventura Fwy (U.S. 101), head south on Ventura Road toward the beach and turn west on Hueneme Road. Follow to Market St.

This unique museum features its own neighborhood! Housed in a quaint 1925 bank building, this refreshingly casual museum of the local world displays personal collections and mementos donated by local residents. The museum highlights the local knowledge that is known to every small community: the shell collection belonging to one neighbor, the salt-and-pepper shakers another collected, a next door neighbor's Indian bead and polished rock collection. There are historical objects from the railroad and soybean industries as well as early Chumash Indian items. There is also a 1984 Olympic torch once carried by a local resident. Exhibits change frequently.

Because it shares the building with the local Chamber of Commerce, this museum is unable to display its total collection at one time, so other community buildings nearby house more exhibits. Bigger museums would call it outreach services, but here they call it "more over at the bank." Tours available by reservation. Annual events include Harbor Days near the Fourth of July. Free street parking. Wheelchair access.

Open weekdays 10 A.M.–4 P.M. Admission is free, but donations are greatly appreciated. For more information call (805) 488-3625 or the Chamber of Commerce at (805) 488-2023, ext. 204.

Santa Barbara Historical Society Museum
136 De La Querra St., Santa Barbara, CA 93102

GETTING THERE: From Ventura Fwy (U.S. 101) take Santa Barbara St. exit north to De La Guerra St.

The Spanish, Mexican, and Early American periods of Santa Barbara's history from the seventeenth to twentieth century are the focus of this small, beautiful museum. The rooms display artifacts and works of art as well as equestrian and farming tools from the Rancho period. A spectacular, large needlepoint illustrating the Rancho Alamo hangs in one room. Also represented in the

Mid-19th century gown and shawl display at the Santa Barbara Historical Society Museum. Courtesy of museum.

Antique dolls from the Trenwith Collection exchange pleasantries over tiny teas at the Santa Barbara Historical Society Museum. Courtesy of museum.

collection is evidence of the era when the Royal Presidio was located in Santa Barbara. Elegant sterling silver stirrups and ladies' sterling silver reins, fans, and costumes are in the Spanish room, along with a beautiful collection of mission paintings by Edwin Deakin. There is an abundant doll collection. One surprising piece is an enormous Chinese shrine, embellished with carved scenes of Chinese mythology and history, a gift to the museum from some former Chinese residents of Santa Barbara. Frequent touring exhibits. Docent-led tours are available on Saturday, Sunday and Wednesday at 1:30 P.M. Annual events include receptions to honor Saint Barbara on December 4, Santa Barbara's birthday (April 21), and a fiesta in late July. Educational services include slide presentations and tours for schools and groups. Reservations required. The gift shop sells museum publications and books on Santa Barbara history, also antique doll reproductions, fans, and stationery. No dining facilities. Wheelchair access.

The historical society also owns and operates the Trussel-Winchester Adobe and the beautiful Victorian Fernald House, both built in the 1880s. Fully furnished, they are open by appointment only. Call (805) 966-1601.

Open Tuesday–Friday noon–5 P.M., Saturday and Sunday 1–5 P.M. Free admission and parking. For more information call (805) 966-1601.

Santa Barbara Museum of Art
1130 State St., Santa Barbara, CA 93101

GETTING THERE: From the Ventura Fwy (U.S. 101) take State St. exit and follow to Anapamu St. in downtown Santa Barbara. The museum is on the corner of State and Anapamu. Turn left into the city parking lot behind the museum.

The beautiful Santa Barbara Museum of Art is considered to be one of the finest regional museums in the United States. Visitors will enjoy the outstanding collections here: fine Chinese ceramics; woodcut prints by Kabayashi Kiyochika, the largest collection outside of Japan; an exquisite array of classical antiquities; and a collection of rare Chinese sculpture.

The central sculpture court contains some of the West Coast's most important Greco-Roman antiquities, mainly gifts from Wright S.

The Santa Barbara Museum of Art is acclaimed throughout the state for its fine collections. Photo by Sara LeBien.

Ludington, including the fourth century B.C. *Funerary Loutrophoros,* and *Torso of Heracles.* First century B.C. works include *Torso of the Doryphoros, Nude Torso of a Youth, Aphrodite,* and an outstanding selection of Greek, Roman and Etruscan bronzes.

Two wings flanking the central building house American art and oriental art. The Chinese collection is comprised mainly of works of the eleventh and twelfth century (Sung) dynasty. The Preston Morton Collection of American Art includes works of George Inness, Thomas Eakins, Winslow Homer, John Singer Sargent, George Bellows, Edward Hopper, and Edgar Sloan. Visitors may also see works by William Merritt Chase, John George Brown, and William Morris Hunt as well as Frederic Remington's 1903 bronze, *The Mountain Man.* Additional permanent collections include oriental painting and porcelain, European and American watercolors, drawings from the Renaissance to present, and the Schott Antique Doll Collection. The museum's print collection includes works by Klee, Corot, Degas, Matisse, and Toulouse-Lautrec. The graphics collection has recently acquired 4,000 French lithographs including nine hundred works by Daumier. A major collection of photographs include most of the notables of twentieth-century photography. Included are works by William Jackson, Edward S. Curtis, Edward Steinchen, and Berenice Abott. Others are by Barbara Morgan, Eliot Proter, Yousuf Karsh, Harry Callahan, Robert Rauschenberg, David Hockney, George Tice, Joan Myers, and Ted Rice.

Besides the changing exhibitions of its permanent collection and traveling exhibitions, the museum offers a full schedule of films, lectures, and live performances presented in the Mary Craig Auditorium. Art education classes are also held at the museum, and "Sunday–Funday" is a family workshop with different themes each week. The art library is open to the public and provides many services for museum members and local educators. These include 40,000 volumes and interlibrary loan plus a circulation of 30,000 slides. Docent tours offered at 2 P.M. daily. "Focus Tours" on special exhibitions are held each Wednesday and Saturday at 1 P.M. Tours for senior citizens and special groups. Slide lectures available for schools and community.

The museum bookstore is said to have the best selection of art books in Santa Barbara plus many periodicals, exhibition catalogs, art jewelry, prints, and drawings. No restaurant, but many can be found along State Street within walking distance. Wheelchair access throughout. There is parking behind the museum in the city lot or along side streets, and there is wheelchair access from the parking lot and throughout the museum.

Open Tuesday–Saturday 11 A.M.–5 P.M., Thursday 11 A.M.–9 P.M., Sunday noon–5 P.M. Admission is free. Special exhibitions may require a fee. For more information call (805) 693-4364.

Santa Barbara Museum of Natural History
2559 Puesta del Sol Road, Santa Barbara, CA 93105

GETTING THERE: From the Ventura Fwy (U.S. 101) take State St. exit to Los Olivos St. then go four blocks toward the mountains. The museum is two blocks north of the mission.

With the ambiance of a rambling Spanish home and nestled in a grove of oak and massive sycamore trees, this natural history museum occupies eleven shady acres in historic Mission Canyon. Its exhibits concentrate on the history of the Santa Barbara area, including the Channel Islands and offshore marine life. Indian Hall displays a number of life-size dioramas of many Chumash ceremonies as well as an outstanding Chumash basket collection. A glass-paneled beehive and models of natural habitats are on display and the museum has comprehensive collections of birds and eggs, Native American pottery and textiles, shells, minerals, and insects.

The permanent collection includes antique prints by John James Audubon, John Gould, and Daniel Elliot; American Indian prints by Karl Bodner and George Catlin; photographs by Edward S. Curtis; also original paintings on paper of Campbell Grant's Chumash rock art. At Stearns Wharf visitors will enjoy the new Sea Center, a satellite facility displaying marine environment exhibits. Research library of 30,000 volumes, planetarium, observatory and research labs. Art and nature workshops. Educational services include afterschool programs and adult education classes, outreach, and hands-on discovery lab. Field trips, including whale watching, Channel Island excursions, nature walks, film series, and special event in the performing arts, as well as planetarium programs and star shows. Tours available for the general public on Sundays at 2 P.M.

The Santa Barbara Museum of Natural History. Photo by Sara LeBien.

"Whale watching" at the Santa Barbara Museum of Natural History. Photo by Sara LeBien.

No restaurant. Picnic area across the street at in Rocky Nook Park. Gift shop sells books, nature gifts, museum-made cards, and crafts. Wheelchair access.

Open weekdays 9 A.M.–5 P.M., Sundays and holidays 10 A.M.–5 P.M. Closed on Thanksgiving, Christmas, New Year's Day, and "Afternoon of the Fiesta." Free admission and parking. Donations appreciated. For more information call (805) 682-4711.

Stagecoach Inn Museum and Tri-Village
51 South Ventura Park Road, Newbury Park, CA 91360

GETTING THERE: Follow the Ventura Fwy (U.S. 101) to Ventu Park Road exit and continue south ¼ mile to a dirt road entrance at a small wooden sign.

The original Stagecoach Inn of 1876 was destroyed by fire in 1970. This two-story replica has eighteen beautifully furnished rooms, some of which are now galleries for touring exhibitions, and others furnished in period decor. On the museum's lower level are exhibits of Chumash Indian pottery and basketry, Chumash rock painting, and several exhibits of the plant and animal life of the Conejo Valley. Adjacent to the inn a small historical village represents the three early settlement eras in the Conejo Valley—a Chumash Indian hut, a Spanish adobe, and an Anglo-pioneer cabin. A carriage house exhibits tools and two stagecoaches. The gift shop sells books and handmade items. Picnic area. Wheelchair access to first floor of inn. Free parking.

Open Wednesday, Thursday, Friday, and Sunday 1–4 P.M. Closed on holidays. The carriage house, village, and lower level are open on Sundays only. Admission is $1 for adults, children and senior citizens 50¢. For more information call (805) 498-9441.

Stow House
304 Los Carneros Road, Goleta, CA 93117

GETTING THERE: Take U.S. 101 to the Los Carneros Road exit (eight miles northwest of Santa Barbara) in Goleta. The museum is behind the fire station near the freeway exit.

Tucked back among enormous pine and oak trees behind the Goleta Depot Museum is the Stow House, one of the oldest

The Stagecoach Inn Museum of Newbury Park. Photo by Sara LeBien.

Stow House (1872), a landmark in Goleta Valley. Photo by Sara LeBien.

landmarks in Goleta Valley. An interesting cluster of historic structures on this former ranch include a bunkhouse, farm museum,
and blacksmith shop. The main attraction is the beautifully furnished house. Built in 1872 on a 1,043-acre ranch, the Victorian era
furnishings include wedding gowns dating from the 1830s to 1950s,
an unusual portable French piano designed to be used at sea, a
speaking tube intercom from the second floor to the first, and
much more. The original bunkhouse now serves as an historic
library and the former packing house for the ranch's almond, walnut, and lemon crops is now a museum of early ranching memorabilia. In addition is the large blacksmith shop furnished with
equipment used in servicing the farm machinery and forging handwrought ironwork. Tours available on selected holidays and weekends. Annual events at the ranch include an antique auto and
engine show, "Grandma's Attic" sale on the first Sunday in March,
"Spelling Bee" in May, a barbecue on the first Sunday in June, an
old-fashioned elaborate Fourth of July celebration, a fiddler's convention on the second Sunday in October, and a Christmas open
house. School tours available. Free parking at the Goleta Depot
Railroad Museum nearby. Picnic area. No wheelchair facilities.

Open Saturday and Sunday 2–4 P.M. from Memorial Day through Labor Day. Open
during the remainder of the year on Sunday 2–4 P.M. Admission is free and donations are appreciated. For more information call (805) 964-4407.

Strathearn Historical Park
137 Strathearn Place, Simi Valley, CA 93065

GETTING THERE: From the Simi Valley-San Fernando Valley
Fwy (118) drive to the west end of the Simi Valley and exit at
Madera Road. Drive south to Strathearn Place and turn right.

This "living local history museum" portrays the domestic and farm
life of the 1870s. The finest historical feature here is the Simi
Adobe, headquarters for El Rancho Simi which was granted in
1795. Remains of an early Chumash Indian village with two
Victorian houses display many domestic items and two barns contain farming implements of that era. The main house belonged to
the largest land-owning family in Simi Valley. Exhibits pertain to
daily life of early settlers, especially toolmaking and the art of quilting and spinning. Annual events include a barn dance fundraiser

in September, Christmas decor during holidays. School tours and research assistance available. Tours available. Call for reservations.

Also on site is the façade of a barn used in the television series "Little House on the Prairie" which was filmed in Simi Valley's Tapo Canyon. Gift shop, no food services. Limited wheelchair access.

Open Sundays 1–4 P.M. Closed during wet weather. Free admission and parking. For more information call (805) 526–6453.

University Art Museum, Santa Barbara
University of California, Santa Barbara, CA 93106

GETTING THERE: Take Ventura Fwy (U.S. 101) through Santa Barbara to Los Carneros Road exit. Turn south to the University entrance. A parking lot attendant will provide a campus map and instructions.

Housed in the Arts Building on the UC–Santa Barbara campus, this museum has two galleries showing permanent collections, a large space devoted to changing exhibitions, and a small outdoor sculpture garden. The Sedgwick Gallery includes paintings by Jacob van Ruisdael, Melchoir de Hondecoeter, Cornelis Mahu, Ludolf Backhuysen, Philips Wouwerman, Bellini, and Juan de Flandes, and religious paintings.

The Sigmund Morgenroth Collection of renaissance medals and plaquettes includes over 400 works largely from the fifteenth and sixteenth century. Made of bronze or fruitwood, they have delicate, detailed scenes with portraits on one side and an image symbolizing the person's achievement on the other side. The Arthur Silver Collection is of tiny terra-cotta heads from Hellenistic Age figurines, each very individualistic and in perfect condition. Africa art, prints and drawings, and contemporary art comprise the rest of the permanent collection.

Tours are available on Saturday at 2 P.M. No reservations necessary. Gift shop has a good selection of art catalogs, art books, posters, cards, gift items related to the exhibitions, and jewelry by art students. Eating facilities are available on the campus. Parking $1 on weekdays, free on weekends. Wheelchair access.

Open Tuesday–Saturday 10 A.M.–4 P.M., Sunday 1–5 P.M. Free admission. For more information call (805) 961-3013.

Ventura County Museum of History and Art
100 East Main St., Ventura, CA 93001

GETTING THERE: Take Ventura Fwy (U.S. 101) to the California St. exit. Go north to Main St. and turn left. The museum is across from the Albinger Archaeological Museum.

This attractive, modern adobe museum features local Ventura history in the main gallery, with major exhibits changing every three years. In another gallery new shows are featured every six to eight weeks on history, archaeology, fine arts, or contemporary works. The Smith Gallery displays a rotating exhibit of the collection of George Stuart's exquisite historical figures. The two hundred life-like one-quarter-size figures represent important historical persons from American, European, and Asian history. Stuart gives a monthly monologue at the museum "talking out their lives." In conjunction with this collection is an excellent display showing the steps taken by Stuart as he designs these unique treasures. The museum also has an early farm machinery display in an outdoor courtyard. Films, lectures, and workshops. Annual events include "Assembly of the Arts" and "Pioneer Picnic." Educational programs include speakers' bureau, visual arts program, school outreach program. Tours available for school and general public by reservation. Reference library of 10,000 photographs pertaining to local history. The gift shop sells handcrafted items from around the world and books on California history. Picnic area. Wheelchair access and parking.

Open Tuesday–Sunday 10 A.M.–5 P.M. Closed Mondays. Free admission and parking. For more information call (805) 653-5469 and (805) 653-0323.

Western States Museum of Photography
1321 Alameda Padre Serra, Santa Barbara, CA 93103

GETTING THERE: The museum is located at the Jefferson campus of the Brooks Institute of Photography. Take the Ventura Fwy (U.S. 101) north to the Salinas St. exit and go straight ahead to Alameda Padre Serra.

Small but significant, this museum is for serious aficionados of photography. One of the largest collections of cameras and camera equipment in the world, dating back to the 1800s, also stereo camera viewers, zoetropes, ambrotypes, and daguerreotypes. All manner of memorabilia having to do with cameras and film processing are exhibited. Large antique cameras of highly polished wood and brass work are set out for close inspection. The museum highlights internationally known photographers and their works in striking exhibits every two months or so. Tours available. Call for reservations. The museum is located high above Santa Barbara and has a spectacular view of the city and coastline. Wheelchair access and parking.

Open daily 10 A.M.–4 P.M. Closed on holidays. Free admission and parking. Donations appreciated. For more information call (805) 965-8664.

An 1886 "spy camera" to be worn under vest with the lens protruding out a buttonhole, on view at the Western States Museum of Photography. Courtesy Brooks Foundation.

Annual Events

Spring

Adobe De Palomares
Adobe Days in March

California Antelope Valley California Poppy Reserve
California Poppy Day on April 16

Casa De Rancho Cucamonga
Old Rancho Days in May

CEC/Seabee Museum
Memorial Service during Memorial Day Week

Channel Islands National Park Museum
Celebration of the Whale and Environmental Fair

Hi-Desert Nature Museum
Wildflower Exhibit

Imperial Valley College Museum
Field Trip and Book Sale

Julian Pioneer Museum
Wildflower Show

Los Encinos State Historic Park
Living History Program

Maiki Museum
Memorial Day Fiesta

Martyrs Memorial and Museum of the Holocaust
Holocaust Memorial Day in April

Mission San Juan Capistrano
"Swallows Day"

Mott Miniatures Collection
Country Fair

Mojave River Valley Museum
Barbecue and Open House in May

Pacific Asia Museum
Food Festival

Planes of Fame Air Museum
Air Show and Open House in May

Queen Mary
Queen Mary Jazz Festival in May

Rancho Los Cerritos Museum
Easter Egg Hunt

John Rowland Home
Wisteria Tea

Santa Barbara Historical Museum
Celebration of Santa Barbara's Birthday on April 21

Southern Pacific Train Depot and Museum of Saugus
Old Town Celebration

Stow House
Antique Auto and Engine Show and Grandma's Attic Sale on first Sunday
in March
Spelling Bee in May

Simon Wiesenthal Center and Museum
Holocaust Memorial Day

Whitaker-Jaynes and Bacon Houses
Old Tyme Picnic on the third Sunday in May

Workman and Temple Homestead
Architectural Crafts Fair in May

Summer

Antique Gas and Steam Engine Museum
Threshing Bees and Antique Engine Show in June

Bolton Hall Museum
July 4th Parade Float

Carpinteria Valley Museum of History
Summer Faire

Centinela Adobe
Barbecue in June

Long Beach Museum of Art
Artists' Market in June

Casa de Geronimo Lopez
Blessing of Fruits and Flowers on the first Sunday in June

Mission San Diego De Alacala
Fiesta of the Bells and Blessing of the Animals in July

Natural History Museum of Los Angeles County
Folk Art Festival

Old Spanish Days Carriage Museum
Participation in the city's Fiesta in late July or first week of August

Olivas Adobe Historical Park
Old Adobe Days

Ontario Museum of History and Art
Permanent Collection Show in July and August

George C. Page Museum of La Brea Discoveries
"Pit 91" Excavation

Port Hueneme Historical Museum
Harbor Days during Fourth of July week

Rancho Los Alamitos Historical Site and Gardens
California Ranch Day in June

Reuben H. Fleet Science Center
National Space Week the second week of July

Riverside Art Museum
Living with Art decorator showhouse and "Fun in the Sun" in June of alternate years

San Diego Museum of Man
Indian Fair the second weekend of June

Santa Barbara Historical Museum
Participation in the city's Fiesta in late July or first week of August

Stow House
Barbecue on first Sunday of June
Fourth of July Celebration

Villa Montezuma/Jesse Shepard House
Participation in "America's Finest City Week" in August

William S. Hart Ranch
Fourth of July parade participation

Fall

Albinger Archaeological Museum
Archaeology Day in November

Andres Pico Adobe
"Rancho Days" in September

Antique Gas and Steam Engine Museum
Threshing Bees and Antique Engine Show in October

Centinela Adobe
Fiesta in September

Conejo Valley Art Museum
Juried Photography Show and Western Art Show during city's "Conejo Days"

Craft and Folk Art Museum
Mask Festival in October

Downey Museum of Art
Art Fair in the Park

Forest Lawn Memorial Park—Hollywood Hills
West Coast Sacred Torch Ceremony on Veteran's Day, November 11

Goleta Depot Railroad Museum
"Depot Day" in October

Imperial Valley College Museum
Field Trip and Book Sale

Lomita Railroad Museum
Ice Cream Social

Mingei International Museum of World Folk Art
"Treasures and Trivia" Folk Art Sale

Mott Miniatures
Halloween Haunt

Museum of Photographic Arts
Awards Exhibition

NASA Ames-Dryden Flight Research Center and Museum
Air Force Open House and Air Show

Point Vicente Museum and Whale Watch Site
Special event each October

Pacific Asia Museum
Festival of the Autumn Moon

John Rowland Home
Barbecue on second Sunday in October

San Diego Aerospace Museum
Model Contest

San Diego Museum of Man
Haunted Museum October 25–31
Rock Art Symposium on first weekend of November

Santa Barbara Museum of Art
Day of the Dead celebration in November

Southwest Museum
Festival of Native American Arts in October

Stow House
Fiddler's Convention on second Sunday in October

Strathearn Historical Park
Barn Dance Fund Raiser in September

Ventura County Museum of History and Art
Pioneer Picnic

Will Rogers State Historic Park
Equestrian Day in October

William S. Hart Ranch Museum
Western Jamboree in September

Winter

Lincoln Memorial Shrine
Open House on February 12

Los Encinos State Historic Park
"Living History" Program

Natural History Museum of Los Angeles County
Behind the Scenes Open House

Ontario Museum of History and Art
Juried Show during January and February

Point Vicente Museum and Whale Watch Site
Whale of a Day in January

San Diego Natural History Museum
Weekend boat trips to view migrating whales in December and January

Santa Barbara Historical Society Museum
Celebration of Saint Barbara on December 4

Christmas

The Bailey House
Christmas Tea

Banning Residence Museum
Victorian Christmas on first Sunday of December

Burbank's Gordon R. Howard Museum
Christmas Party

California Museum of Photography
Photographer's Christmas Card exhibit and open house

Carpinteria Valley Museum of History
Open House in early December and Holiday Faire

Casa de Rancho Cucamonga
Gourmet Christmas Dinner

Centinela Adobe
Christmas Open House

El Monte Museum of History
Christmas Reception

Fontana Farms Camp #1 Museum
Children's Christmas Party

Goleta Depot Railroad Museum
Christmas Party on the last three Saturdays of December

Heritage House
Open House on the second Sunday of December

Heritage House
Victorian Christmas Faire

Hollywood Studio Museum
Holiday Party

Casa de Geronimo Lopez
Christmas Tour

Los Encinos State Historic Park
Victorian Christmas

Natural History Museum of Los Angeles County
Native American Festival

Olivas Adobe Historical Park
Christmas Posada on Christmas Eve

Pasadena Historical Society Museum (Fenyes Mansion)
Edwardian Christmas

Rancho Los Cerritos Museum
1870s Ranch Candlelight Christmas

Rancho Los Alamitos Historic Site and Gardens
Christmas Eve Celebration for three consecutive evenings

John Rowland Home
Christmas Open House

San Diego Hall of Champions
Christmas on the Prado Open House

Santa Monica Heritage Museum
Christmas Toy Show

Southwest Museum
Family Christmas Party

Stow House
Christmas Open House

Villa Montezuma/Jesse Shepard House
Elaborate Christmas decorations

Whittier Narrows Nature Center
Christmas Boutique

Workman and Temple Homestead
Christmas Open House

Museums by Category

Many museums have a little bit of everything in them. This listing indentifies the museums according to their major collections or main focus. Most museums will be listed more than once; some as many as six or seven times, if they have several major diverse installations.

Aerospace *(see also Aviation)*
Aerospace Museum
NASA Ames-Dryden Research Center and Flight Museum
San Diego Aerospace Museum

American Art *(see also Western American and California Art)*
Forest Lawn Memorial-Parks (Hollywood Hills)
Forest Lawn Memorial-Parks (Glendale)
The Huntington Library Art Collections and Botanical Gardens
Los Angeles County Museum of Art
Natural History Museum of Los Angeles County
Newport Harbor Museum
San Diego Museum of Art
Santa Barbara Museum of Art
Timken Art Gallery
UCLA Wight Gallery Complex

American History
Forest Lawn Memorial-Parks (Hollywood Hills)

Lincoln Memorial Shrine
Natural History Museum of Los Angeles County
Ventura County Museum of History and Art

Anthropology *(see also Native American History)*
Albinger Archaeological Museum
Raymond M. Alf Museum
Antelope Valley Indian Museum
Imperial Valley College Museum
Natural History Museum of Los Angeles County
Riverside Municipal Museum
San Diego Museum of Man
Skirball Museum of the Hebrew Union College

Antiquities
J. Paul Getty Art Museum
Los Angeles County Museum of Art
San Diego Museum of Art
Santa Barbara Museum of Art

Animals *(see also Marine)*
Greater Los Angeles Zoo
Placerita Canyon Nature Center
San Diego Zoo
Whittier Narrows Museum and Wildlife Sanctuary

Architectural Sites *(see also Historic Buildings)*
Banning Residence Museum
The Doctor's House
Frank Lloyd Wright's Hollyhock House

J. Paul Getty Art Museum
Heritage Square
Charles F. Lummis Home
Villa Montezuma/Jesse Shepard
  House

Asian Art *(see also Cultural Art)*
Los Angeles County Museum of
  Art
Pacific Asia Museum
San Diego Museum of Art
Santa Barbara Museum of Art

Automobiles and Other Vehicles
Burbank's Gordon R. Howard
  Museum
Merle Norman Classic Beauty Col-
  lections at San Sylmar
Natural History Museum of Los
  Angeles County
Old Spanish Days Carriage
  Museum
Stagecoach Inn Museum and
  Tri-Village

Aviation
Aeropsace Museum
Burbank's Gordon R. Howard
  Museum
Donald Douglas Museum and
  Library
March Field Museum
NASA Ames-Dryden Research
  Center and Flight Museum
Planes of Fame Air Museum
San Diego Aerospace Museum
Spruce Goose Flying Boat

**Botanical Gardens and Plant
Exhibits**
Adobe de Palomares
Antelope Valley California Poppy
  Reserve
Greater Los Angeles Zoo
Historic George Key Museum
The Huntington Library Art
  Collections and Botanical
  Gardens
Kimberly Crest House and
  Gardens
Los Angeles County Arboretum
Mission San Gabriel
Mission San Juan Capistrano
  Museum
Mission Santa Barbara

Rancho Los Cerritos Museum
Rancho Los Alamitos Historic Site
  and Gardens

California Art
Carnegie Art Museum
Laguna Art Museum
Long Beach Museum of Art
Museum of Contemporary Art
  and Temporary Contemporary
Newport Harbor Museum
Ontario Museum of History and
  Art
Riverside Art Museum

California History
Adobe de Palomares
Andres Pico Adobe
Antique Gas and Steam Engine
  Museum
Cabrillo National Monument
Carpinteria Valley Museum of
  History
Casa de Rancho Cucamonga
Dominguez Rancho Adobe
El Molino Viejo Museum
El Monte Museum of History
El Pueblo de Los Angeles State
  Historic Park
Fontana Farms Camp #1 Museum
The Fullerton Museum Center
Heritage Hill Historic Park
Mission San Diego de Alcala
Mission San Fernando Rey de
  España
Mission San Gabriel
Mission San Juan Capistrano
  Museum
Mission Santa Barbara
Natural History Museum of Los
  Angeles County
Rancho Los Alamitos Historic Site
  and Gardens
Rancho Los Cerritos Museum
Santa Barbara Historical Society
  Museum
Junipero Serra Museum
Stagecoach Inn Museum and
  Tri-Village
Strathearn Historical Park
Ventura County Museum of
  History and Art
Wells Fargo History Museum
Whitaker-Jaynes and Bacon
  Houses

Children's *(see also Participatory)*
Anaheim Museum
Children's Museum at La Habra
Children's Museum of San Diego
Los Angeles Children's Museum
San Bernardino County Museum

Contemporary Art
Downey Museum of Art
Laguna Art Museum
La Jolla Museum of Contemporary
Art
Long Beach Museum of Art
Museum of Contemporary Art
and Temporary Contemporary
Newport Harbor Museum
Palm Springs Desert Museum
Riverside Art Museum
San Diego Museum of Art
UCLA Wight Gallery Complex
University Art Museum, Long
Beach
University Art Museum, Santa
Barbara

Cultural Art
Bowers Museum
California Museum of Afro-
American History and Culture
Conejo Valley Art Museum
Craft and Folk Art Museum
The Fenyes House
The Fullerton Museum Center
Los Angeles County Museum of
Art
Martyrs Memorial and Museum of
the Holocaust
Mingei International Museum of
Folk Art
Mission Santa Barbara
Skirball Museum of the Hebrew
Union College
Southwest Museum and Casa de
Adobe
UCLA Museum of Cultural
History
University Art Museum, Santa
Barbara

Cultural History
Bowers Museum
California Museum of Afro-
American History and Culture
The Fullerton Museum Center

Martyrs Memorial and Museum of
the Holocaust
Museum of Mexican History and
Plaza of Mexican Heritage
UCLA Museum of Cultural
History
Simon Wiesenthal Center and
Museum

Decorative Arts
Edward-Dean Museum of Decora-
tive Arts
Forest Lawn Memorial-Parks
(Glendale)
J. Paul Getty Art Museum
Kimberly Crest House and
Gardens
Malibu Lagoon Museum
Workman and Temple Homestead

Economics
Mark Taper Hall of Economics
and Finance

European Art
Edward-Dean Museum of Decora-
tive Arts
Forest Lawn Memorial-Parks
(Glendale)
J. Paul Getty Art Museum
The Huntington Library Art
Collections and Botanical
Gardens
Los Angeles County Museum of
Art
San Diego Museum of Art
Norton Simon Museum
Timken Art Gallery
UCLA Wight Gallery Complex
University Art Museum, Santa
Barbara

Folk Art *(see also Cultural Art)*
Craft and Folk Art Museum
Mingei International Museum of
World Folk Art
Pasadena Historical Society
Museum
UCLA Museum of Cultural
History

Glass
Historical Glass Museum

Graphic Arts

Grunwald Center for Graphic Arts
Santa Barbara Museum of Art

Health

Kinsey Hall of Health Sciences

Historic Buildings (see also Architectural Sites)

Adobe de Palomores
George Anderson House
Andres Pico Adobe
Bailey House
Banning Residence House
Bolton Hall Museum
Burbank's Gordon R. Howard Museum
Casa Adobe de San Rafael
Casa de Geronimo Lopez
Casa de Rancho Cucamonga
Centinela Adobe
The Doctor's House
Dominguez Rancho Adobe
El Molino Viejo Museum
El Pueblo de Los Angeles State Historic Park
The Fenyes House
Fontana Farms Camp #1 Museum
Frank Lloyd Wright's Hollyhock House
The Fullerton Museum Center
The Gamble House
Goleta Depot Railroad Museum
Heritage Hill Historical Park
Heritage House
Heritage Square
Historic George Key Ranch
Hollywood Studio Museum
Julian Pioneer Museum
Kimberly Crest House and Gardens
Leonis Adobe and Plummer House
Los Angeles County Arboretum
Los Encinos State Historical Park
Charles F. Lummis Home
Malibu Lagoon Museum
Mission San Diego de Alcala
Mission San Fernando Rey de España
Mission San Gabriel
Mission San Juan Capistrano Museum
Mission Santa Barbara

Old Town San Diego State Historic Park
Olivas Adobe Historical Park
Ontario Museum of History and Art
Ortega Adobe
Rancho Los Alamitos Historic Site and Gardens
Rancho Los Cerritos Museum
John Rowland Historic Home
Santa Monica Heritage Museum
Junipero Serra Museum
Sherman Indian Museum
Southern Pacific Train Depot and Museum of Saugus
Southwest Museum and Casa de Adobe
Stagecoach Inn Museum and Tri-Village
Stow House
Strathearn Historical Park
Villa Montezuma
Whitaker-Jaynes and Bacon Houses
Whittier Historical Museum
Will Rogers State Historic Park
Workman and Temple Homestead

Indian (see Native American History)

Industry

Anaheim Museum
Antique Gas and Steam Engine Museum
Burbank's Gordon R. Howard Museum
California Museum of Science and Industry
Carpinteria Valley Museum of History
Donald Douglas Museum and Library
El Molino Viejo Museum
Fillmore Historical Museum
The Fullerton Museum Center
Historic George Key Ranch
Historical Glass Museum
Hollywood Studio Museum
Malibu Lagoon Museum
Ojai Valley Museum and Historical Society
Wells Fargo History Museum

Local History (see also Native American History, California History)

Anaheim Museum
George Anderson House
Bolton Hall Museum
Bowers Museum
Burbank's Gordon R. Howard
Museum
Cabrillo National Monument
Carpinteria Valley Museum of
History
Casa de Rancho Cucamonga
Catalina Island Museum
Centinela Adobe
Channel Islands National Park
The Fenyes House
Fillmore Historical Museum
Heritage Hill Historical Park
- Historic George Key Ranch
Hollywood Bowl Museum
Imperial Valley Pioneers Museum
Julian Pioneer Museum
Leonis Adobe and Plummer
House
Los Angeles Valley College Histor-
ical Museum
Malibu Lagoon Museum
Mission San Diego de Alcala
Mission San Juan Capistrano
Mojave River Valley Museum
Ojai Valley Museum and Histori-
cal Society
Old Town San Diego State
Historic Park
Olivas Adobe Historic Park
Ontario Museum of History and
Art
Placerita Canyon Nature Center
Point Vicente Interpretive Center
Port Hueneme Historical Museum
Riverside Municipal Museum
San Bernardino County Museum
Santa Barbara Historical Society
Museum
Santa Monica Heritage Museum
Junipero Serra Museum
Southern Pacific Train Depot and
Museum of Saugus
Stagecoach Inn Museum and
Tri-Village
Strathearn Historical Park
Ventura County Museum of His-
tory and Art
Whittier Historical Museum
Whittier Narrows Museum and
Wildlife Sanctuary

Marine
Cabrillo Marine Museum
Channel Islands National Park
Point Vicente Interpretive Center
Santa Barbara Natural History
Museum
Scripps Aquarium/Museum
Sea World

Maritime
Catalina Island Museum
Los Angeles Maritime Museum
Nautical Heritage Museum
The *Queen Mary*
Star of India

Military
American Heritage Park/Military
Museum
CEA/Seabee Museum
Drum Barracks Civil War Museum
Fort MacArthur Military Museum

Miniatures
Angel's Attic
Mott Miniatures

Motion Pictures
Hollywood Studio Museum

Music
Hollywood Bowl Museum
Merle Norman Classic Beauty Col-
lections at San Sylmar

Native American History *(see also
Anthropology)*
Albinger Archaeological Museum
Andres Pico Adobe
Antelope Valley Indian Museum
Carpinteria Valley Museum of
History
Casa de Rancho Cucamonga
Imperial Valley Pioneers Museum
Julian Pioneer Museum
Maiki Museum
Malibu Lagoon Museum
Mission San Diego de Alcala
Mission San Juan Capistrano
Museum
Natural History Museum of Los
Angeles County
Natural History Museum of
Orange County

Ojai Valley Museum and Histori-
cal Society
Riverside Municipal Museum
San Diego Museum of Man
Santa Barbara Museum of Natural
History
Sherman Indian Museum
Southwest Museum and Casa de
Adobe
Stagecoach Inn Museum and
Tri-Village

Natural History
Raymond M. Alf Museum
Antelope Valley California Poppy
Reserve
Hi-Desert Nature Museum
Mojave River Valley Museum
Natural History Museum of Los
Angeles County
Natural History Museum of
Orange County
Ojai Valley Museum and Histori-
cal Society
Palm Springs Desert Museum
Placerita Canyon Nature Center
Riverside Municipal Museum
San Bernardino County Museum
San Diego Natural History
Museum
Santa Barbara Museum of Natural
History
Scripps Aquarium/Museum
Whittier Narrows Museum and
Wildlife Sanctuary

Neon Art
Museum of Neon Art

Paleontology
Raymond M. Alf Museum
Imperial Valley College Museum
Natural History Museum of Los
Angeles County
Natural History Museum of
Orange County
George C. Page Museum of La
Brea Discoveries
San Bernardino County Museum
San Diego Museum of Natural
History

Participatory
Aerospace Museum
Anaheim Museum
California Museum of Science and
Industry

Children's Museum at La Habra
Children's Museum of San Diego
Kinsey Hall of Health Sciences
Los Angeles Children's Museum
Reuben H. Fleet Space Theater
and Science Center
Mark Taper Hall of Economics
and Finance

Performing Arts
Hollywood Bowl Museum

Personal History
William S. Hart Ranch and
Museum
Charles F. Lummis Home
Roy Rogers and Dale Evans
Museum
Villa Montezuma/Jesse Shephard
House
Will Rogers State Historic Park

Photography
California Museum of
Photography
J. Paul Getty Art Museum
Grunwald Center for Graphic Arts
Museum of Photographic Art
Santa Barbara Museum of Art
Western States Museum of
Photography
Railroad
Goleta Depot Railroad Museum
Lomita Railroad Museum
San Diego Model Railroad
Museum
Southern Pacific Train Depot and
Museum of Saugus
Travel Town Transportation
Museum

Religious Art
Forest Lawn Memorial-Parks
(Glendale)
Mission San Fernando Rey de
España
Mission San Gabriel
Mission Santa Barbara
Skirball Museum of the Hebrew
Union College
Timken Art Gallery

Science
California Museum of Science and
Industry
The Fullerton Museum Center
Griffith Observatory/Museum

IMAX Theater
Reuben H. Fleet Space Theater
and Science Center

Sculpture
California Museum of Afro-
American History and Culture
J. Paul Getty Art Museum
Laguna Art Museum
La Jolla Museum of Contemporary
Art
Long Beach Art Museum
Los Angeles County Museum of
Art
The Modern Museum of Art
Franklin D. Murphy Sculpture
Garden
Museum of Contemporary Art
and Temporary Contemporary
Palm Springs Desert Museum
San Diego Museum of Art
Santa Barbara Museum of Art
Norton Simon Museum
University Art Museum, Long
Beach
University Art Museum, Santa
Barbara

Sports
San Diego Hall of Champions

Theaters
IMAX Theater
Reuben H. Fleet Space Theater
and Science Center

Wax
Hollywood Wax Museum
Movieland Wax Museum

Western American Art
Bowers Museum
Gene Autry Western Heritage
Museum
Palm Springs Desert Museum
Southwest Museum
Will Rogers State Historical Park

Western American History *(see
also California History)*
Gene Autry Western Heritage
Museum
William S. Hart Ranch and
Museum
Old Town San Diego State
Historic Park *(Seeley Stables)*

239

Index of Museums